THE RIOT REPORT

THE RIOT REPORT

A shortened version of the
*Report of the National Advisory
Commission on Civil Disorders*

By BARBARA RITCHIE

Illustrated with photographs

Introduction by Dr. Jeanne Noble

THE VIKING PRESS   NEW YORK

ALEXANDER HAMILTON HIGH SCHOOL
LIBRARY
Elmsford, New York

Copyright © 1969 by Barbara Ritchie. All rights reserved. First published in 1969 by The Viking Press, Inc., 625 Madison Avenue, New York, N. Y. 10022. Published simultaneously in Canada by The Macmillan Company of Canada Limited. Library of Congress catalog card number: 69–18261. Printed in U.S.A. by Rae Publishing Co.

301.45

PHOTOGRAPH CREDITS

Gene Bane (FPG), 2–3; Sheldon Brody (FPG), 138 bottom, 205; Eric Brown (Monkmeyer), 156; Brown Brothers, 95 bottom, 179, 183; Patrick Burns (New York *Times*), 127 bottom; Paul Conklin (Pix), 188–89, 231 bottom; Joe Covello (Black Star), 134–35; Leon Deller (Monkmeyer), 239; Sam Falk (Pictorial Parade), 67; Benedict Fernandez, 37, 46, 51; Toje Fujihira (Monkmeyer), 236; Campbell Hays (Monkmeyer), 172, 194; Ken Heyman, 59 top, 64–65, 167, 191, 218–19, 222, 241; Don Hunstein (Alpha), 146–47; London *Daily Express* (Pictorial Parade), 23; Dan McCoy (Black Star), 160–61; Henry Monroe (Pix), 231 top; Charles Moore (Black Star), 21, 138 top; Joseph Nettis (FPG), 72; New York Historical Society, 87; Paris *Match* (Pictorial Parade), 27; Pictorial Parade, 71, 122; Ernest Reshovsky (Pix), 208–9; Jacob Riis, Museum of the City of New York, 176–77; Frank Rockstroh (Pix), 68 top; Aaron Rosenberg (Alpha), 143; St. Louis *Post Dispatch* (Black Star), 227; Richard Saunders (Pictorial Parade), 118; The Schomburg Collection, New York Public Library, 74–75, 80, 83, 85, 91, 95 top, 103 bottom; Jim Seymour (Pix), 68 bottom; Robert Simmons (Pix), 106–7, 112; United Press International, 29, 56–57, 59 bottom, 97, 103 top, 108, 115, 127 top, 132, 212; Washington *Reporters* (Pix), 40; Wide World, 18–19, 34–35, 45, 202.

Contents

Introduction: "Riders on the Earth Together" — 5
Foreword — 11
The Commission's Task — 12

PART I: WHAT HAPPENED?

The Movement Apart — 18
Detroit: A Profile of Violence — 34
Search for a Pattern — 56

PART II: WHY DID IT HAPPEN?

The Basic Causes — 64
The Negro in America: A Historical Sketch — 74
The Growth of a Movement — 106
How to Build a Ghetto — 134
The Disorganized Society — 146
Life in the Racial Ghetto — 160
"We" Made It, Why Can't "They"? — 176

PART III: WHAT CAN BE DONE?

The Community and the Poor 188
Community Response to Disorder 208
The Future of the Cities 218
Appendix 244
Suggestions for Further Reading 247
Index 251

"Riders on the Earth Together"

"Our nation is moving toward two societies, one black, one white—separate and unequal," concluded the National Advisory Commission on Civil Disorders.

"To see the earth as it truly is, small and blue and beautiful in the eternal silence where it floats, is to see ourselves as riders on the earth together . . . brothers who know how they are truly brothers," wrote the poet Archibald MacLeish in response to the *Apollo* astronauts' view of our beautiful but oh so fragile earth.

How painfully different are these conclusions. How is it that men can orbit the moon and humbly pray for brotherhood, while we foot-drag here on earth in ever-widening circles of racial divisiveness and conflict?

Yet this is the paradox of America as told in this report. As a nation rich in natural, intellectual, and material genius, we have become great at unraveling nature's mysteries. And we grow greater all the time. As a nation dedicated to the ideals of brotherhood and equality, however, we stand before the world a spiritually and morally underdeveloped nation.

The reconciliation of the richness and poverty of our national being is the most urgent problem facing us today. The task to which the Riot Commission summons us calls for "national action—compassionate, massive, and sustained, backed by the resources of the most powerful nation on earth. From every American it will require new attitudes, new understandings, and above all, new will."

The request for new attitudes begins with the hope that youth—as one of the nation's resources—will read the Report with an open mind. During the months since the Report was issued, some Americans have reacted with the kind of old attitudes people often show when they are upset and threatened. Let us examine a few. Some detractors have discredited the authors and the data. They seem to overlook the fact that the study was directed by a bipartisan group of distinguished Americans with moderate social views. Furthermore, scholars have found the methodology and research which led to the conclusions sound.

Another negative attitude is shown when people criticize the language of the Report, calling it excessive and inflammatory—particularly the words "white racism." The Commission claimed that "white racism is essentially responsible for the explosive mixture which has been accumulating in our cities since World War II." These people protest that they are not racists; after all they have never lynched anyone, or refused to sit by a black person on a bus, and, they will tell you, "Some of my best friends are . . ." Others refuse to accept a share of the collective guilt for the widespread injustices described in the Report. They see racism as an individual problem.

Still another reaction is of ebullient approval, which nevertheless seldom moves people to action. This group accepts the words of the Report, even contributing to the rhetoric. Yet they fail to get the meaning. This is especially true of whites who run to the black communities crying: "Guilt! Guilt! We are racists!" Unfortunately, they alienate other whites and fail to move blacks. They miss the simple implications of the Report. Well-meaning whites must communicate with other whites. White racism is a white problem. Until all whites face this fact, blacks will occupy themselves with strategies for survival in a land which they view as hostile and unjust. The Report was not intended as a cathartic outlet; its ultimate message is *action*.

Finally, there is the attitude of "I told you so" as demonstrated by those blacks who are satisfied to see at last the persuasive facts of white racism mirrored before whites by a predominantly white Commission. They fail to ponder these words: "Violence cannot build a better society. Disruption and disorder nourish repression, not justice." If there is no goal to pursue except vengeance, then we aggrieved blacks shall bring nothing of value to the auguries of the human condition. In the end, victim and victor must face each other and heed the words of the philosopher: "I am you and you are me; what have we done to each other?"

There is, on the favorable side, considerable acceptance of the Report. Young Americans, particularly, find it a challenge and blueprint for their energy, idealism, and social consciousness. And it is important that young people respond to this report in these specific ways.

White youth, regardless of personal beliefs, must have the courage to seek out other whites of opposing views. Institutionalized racism as compared to individual prejudice must be recognized, and collective action taken to change our social institutions. The insensitivity of powerful groups in developing negative concepts of self among blacks must be confronted. The social and economic conditions which lead to black alienation from the American mainstream must be explored in the classroom—and young people must insist upon this in their education. The black man has been an invisible man, an inaudible man, all the while saying, "Nobody knows my name." From being perceived as nothing throughout history to proclaiming oneself today as somebody is a long jump. Onlookers often get confused and thwart constructive efforts to achieve this identity. It is often difficult for whites to accept the intense and sometimes frenzied pursuit of black consciousness, especially if, in celebrating his blackness and cultivating those parts of himself that cannot possibly be mistaken for white, the black man turns against some parts of the white experience. But I know no other path toward capturing one's identity from the ruins of history. In this process there is a need for sympathetic advocates. The Commission's report can help make this case.

Black and white youth will find support in this document for black studies programs now being debated in the country. History has unfairly weighted the scales so that whites are favored and blacks discredited. The quest to pick up the historical pieces and rebuild a black identity will continue to preoccupy black youth. Lack of materials, the withholding of community support, and open hostility can prolong and frustrate this process. With patience and cooperation, black young people can and must be encouraged anew to work toward realistic goals of integration.

Black and white youth can and must keep the channels of communication open between themselves. One way to heal divisiveness is to unite around common concerns and projects.

In the final analysis, young people must be active agents for change in the schools and communities, using this document to raise questions concerning the kind of America they want to live in and are surely soon to lead. Youth must raise with each other very fundamental questions: What is the meaning of existence? What will it matter if we land a man on the moon while our brothers cannot walk the street free of physical fear here on earth?

We cannot long tolerate a movement toward two nations, one black, one white—separate and unequal. As separate as we might become, there looms the surety that a common humanity levels us all. We still face the existential facts of birthing, loving, living, and dying in an uncommonly common way. And black and white—though beautiful in their differences—are really only masks for the human condition that joins us all. We are doomed to live this existence together, or not at all. We are bound to seek our answers not in ourselves alone, but in each other. The major goal is indeed "the creation of a true union, a single society and a single American identity." Now we must make of this land a place where all God's children can live humanely as "riders on the earth together."

January 1969

DR. JEANNE NOBLE
Professor of Human Relations
New York University

Foreword

This report of the National Advisory Commission on Civil Disorders responds to Executive Order 11365, issued by President Lyndon B. Johnson on July 29, 1967, and to the personal charge given to us by the President.

"Let your search," he said, "be free. . . . As best you can, find the truth and express it in your report."

We have sought to do so.

"This matter," he said, "is far, far too important for politics."

This was a bipartisan commission and a nonpartisan effort.

"Only you," he said, "can do this job. Only if you . . . put your shoulders to the wheel can America hope for the kind of report it needs and will take to its heart."

This has been a working commission.

To our staff . . . and to all those in government and private life who helped us, we are grateful.

Otto Kerner, Chairman
John V. Lindsay, Vice Chairman
Fred R. Harris
Edward W. Brooke
James C. Corman
William M. McCulloch

I. W. Abel
Charles B. Thornton
Roy Wilkins
Katherine G. Peden
Herbert Jenkins

The Commission's Task

The summer of 1967 again brought racial disorder to American cities, deepening the bitter residue of fear and threatening the future of all Americans.

We are charged by the President with the responsibility of examining this condition and speaking the truth as we see it. Two fundamental questions confront us:

How can we, as a people, end the resort to violence while we build a better society?

How can the nation realize the promise of a single society —one nation indivisible—which yet remains unfulfilled?

We have worked together these past months with a sense of the greatest urgency. Although much remains that can be learned, we have determined to say now, early in March of 1968, what we already have learned. We do this in the hope that the American public will understand the nature and gravity of the problem and that those who have power to act—at all levels of government and in all sections of the community—will listen and respond. Our sense of urgency has led us to consolidate in a single report the interim and final reports called for by the President. We believe that to wait until midsummer of 1968 to present our findings and recommendations may be to forfeit whatever opportunity exists for this report to affect this year the dangerous climate of tension and apprehension that pervades our cities.

During the summer of 1967 over 150 cities reported disorders in Negro—and in some instances, Puerto Rican—neighborhoods. These ranged from minor disturbances to major outbursts involving sustained and widespread looting and destruction of property. The worst came during a two-week period in July when large-scale disorders erupted, first in Newark and then in Detroit, each setting off a chain reaction in neighboring communities.

It was in this troubled and turbulent setting that the President of the United States established this Commission. He called upon it "to guide the country through a thicket of tension, conflicting evidence, and extreme opinions." In his charge the President framed the Commission's mandate in these words:

We need to know the answers to three basic questions about these riots:

What happened?

Why did it happen?

What can be done to prevent it from happening again and again?

In formulating our answers to these questions in this report, we have attempted to draw on all relevant sources. During closed hearings held from August through December 1967 we heard over 130 witnesses. These included Federal, state, and local officials; experts from the military establishment and law-enforcement agencies, universities and foundations; Negro leaders; and representatives of the business community. We personally visited eight cities in which major disturbances had occurred. We met together for twenty-four days to review and revise the several drafts of the report. Through our staff we also undertook field surveys in twenty-three cities in which disorders occurred during the summer of 1967. Sworn testimony was taken in nine of the cities investigated, and from Negro leaders and militants across the country. Expert consultants and advisers supplemented the work of our staff in all the areas covered in our report.

Much of the report is directed to the condition of those Americans who are also Negroes, and to the social and economic environment in which they live—many in the black ghettos of our cities. But this nation is confronted with the issue of justice for all its people—white as well as black, rural as well as urban. In particular, we are concerned for those who have continued to keep faith with society in the preservation of public order—the people of Spanish surname, the American Indians, and other minority groups to whom this country owes much.

We wish it to be clear that in focusing on the Negro we do not mean to imply any priority of need. It will not do to fight misery in the black ghetto and leave untouched the reality of injustice and deprivation elsewhere in our society. The first priority is order and justice for all Americans.

When we speak of the Negro, we do not speak of "them," we speak of *us*; for the freedoms and opportunities of all Americans are diminished and imperiled when they are denied to some Americans.

Two premises underlie the work of the Commission:

This nation cannot abide violence and disorder if it is to ensure the safety of its people and their progress in a free society.

This nation deserves neither safety nor progress unless it can demonstrate the wisdom and the will to undertake decisive action against the root causes of racial disorder.

The report is addressed to the institutions of government and to the conscience of the nation, but even more urgently to the mind and heart of each citizen.

The responsibility for decisive action, never more clearly demanded in the history of our country, rests on all of us. We believe that the likelihood of disorder can be markedly lessened by an American commitment to confront the conditions underlying the disorders and eliminate them—a commitment so clear that Negro citizens will know its truth and accept its goal.

The most important step toward domestic peace is an act of will; this country can do for its people what it chooses to do.

PART I: WHAT HAPPENED?

The Movement Apart

Racial disorder in American cities in the summer of 1967 brought shock, fear, and bewilderment to the nation. In investigating the disorders, we have visited the riot cities; we have heard many witnesses; we have sought the counsel of experts across the country.

This is our basic conclusion: Our nation is moving toward two societies, one black, one white—separate and unequal.

Reaction to the 1967 disorders has quickened the movement and deepened the division. Discrimination and segregation have long permeated much of American life; they now threaten the future of every American.

This deepening racial division is not inevitable. The movement apart can be reversed. Choice is still possible. Our principal task is to define that choice and to press for a national resolution.

To pursue our present course will involve the continuing

polarization of the American community and, ultimately, the destruction of basic democratic values.

The alternative is not blind repression or capitulation to lawlessness. It is the realization of common opportunities for all within a single society.

This alternative will require a commitment to national action—compassionate, massive, and sustained, backed by the resources of the most powerful and richest nation on this earth. From every American it will require new attitudes, new understanding, and above all, new will.

The vital needs of the nation must be met; hard choices must be made and, if necessary, new taxes enacted.

Violence cannot build a better society. Disruption and disorder nourish repression, not justice. They strike at the freedom of every citizen. The community cannot—it will not—tolerate coercion and mob rule.

Violence and destruction must be ended—in the streets of the ghetto and in the lives of people.

Segregation and poverty have created in the racial ghetto a destructive environment totally unknown to most white Americans. What white Americans have never fully understood—but what the Negro can never forget—is that white society is deeply implicated in the ghetto. White institutions created it, white institutions maintain it, and white society condones it.

It is now time to turn with all the purpose at our command to the major unfinished business of this nation. It is time to adopt strategies for action that will produce quick and visible progress. It is time to make good the promises of American democracy to all the citizens—whether urban or rural, white or black, American Indian, of Spanish surname, or any other minority group.

The summer of 1967 was not the beginning of the wave of disorders that is the subject of the Commission's report. Omens of violence had appeared much earlier.

1963–64 In 1963 serious disorders, involving both whites and Negroes, broke out in Birmingham, Alabama; Savannah, Georgia; Cambridge, Maryland; Chicago, and Philadelphia. Sometimes the mobs battled each other; more often they fought the police.

The most violent encounters took place in Birmingham. Police used dogs, fire hoses, and cattle prods against marchers, many of whom were children. White racists shot at Negroes and bombed Negro residences. Negroes retaliated by burning white-owned businesses in Negro areas. On a quiet Sunday morning, a bomb exploded beneath a

Police dogs in Birmingham, 1963

Negro church. Four young girls in a Sunday-school class were killed.

In the spring of 1964 the arrest and conviction of civil-rights demonstrators provoked violence in Jacksonville, Florida. A shot fired from a passing car killed a Negro woman. When a bomb threat forced evacuation of an all-Negro high school, the students stoned policemen and firemen, and burned the cars of newsmen. For the first time, Negroes used Molotov cocktails in setting fires.

Two weeks later, at a demonstration protesting school segregation in Cleveland, a bulldozer accidentally killed a young white minister. When police moved in to disperse a crowd composed primarily of Negroes, violence erupted.

In late June white segregationists broke through police lines and attacked civil-rights demonstrators in St. Augustine, Florida. In Philadelphia, Mississippi, law-enforcement officers were implicated in the lynch murders of three civil-rights workers. On July 10 Ku Klux Klansmen shot and killed a Negro United States Army lieutenant colonel, Lemuel Penn, as he was driving through Georgia.

On July 16, in New York City, several young Negroes walking to summer-school classes became involved in a dispute with a white building superintendent. When an off-duty police lieutenant intervened, a fifteen-year-old boy attacked him with a knife. The officer shot and killed the boy.

A crowd of teen-agers gathered and smashed store windows. Police arrived in force and dispersed the group.

On the following day the Progressive Labor Movement, a Marxist-Leninist organization, printed and passed out inflammatory leaflets charging the police with brutality.

On the second day after the shooting a rally called by the Congress of Racial Equality to protest the Mississippi lynch murders developed into a march on a precinct police station.

Pickets protesting the shooting of a Negro boy by a white policeman in New York, 1964

The crowd clashed with the police; one person was killed, and twelve police officers and nineteen citizens were injured.

For several days thereafter the pattern was repeated. Despite exhortations of Negro community leaders against violence, protest rallies became uncontrollable. Police battled mobs in Harlem and in the Bedford-Stuyvesant section of Brooklyn. Firemen fought fires started with Molotov cocktails. When bricks and bottles were thrown, police responded with gunfire. Widespread looting followed and many persons were injured.

A week later a riot broke out in Rochester, New York, when police tried to arrest an intoxicated Negro youth at a street dance. After two days of violence the National Guard restored order.

During the first two weeks of August disorders took place in three New Jersey communities: Jersey City, Elizabeth, and Paterson.

On August 15, when a white liquor-store owner in the Chicago suburb of Dixmoor had a Negro woman arrested for stealing a bottle of whiskey, he was accused of having manhandled her. A crowd gathered in front of the store, broke the store window, and threw rocks at passing cars. The police restored order. The next day, when the disturbance was renewed, a Molotov cocktail set the liquor store afire. Several persons were injured.

The final violence of the summer occurred in Philadelphia. A Negro couple's car stalled at an intersection in an area known as The Jungle—where, with almost two thousand persons living in each block, there is the greatest incidence of crime, disease, unemployment, and poverty in the city. When two police officers, one white and one black, attempted to move the car, the wife of the owner became abusive, and the officers arrested her. Police officers and Negro spectators gathered at the scene. Two nights of rioting, resulting in extensive damage, followed.

1965 In the spring of 1965 the nation's attention shifted back to the South. When civil-rights workers staged a nonviolent demonstration in Selma, Alabama, police and state troopers forcibly interrupted their march. Within the next few weeks racists murdered a white clergyman and a white housewife active in civil rights.

In the small Louisiana town of Bogalusa, when Negro demonstrators attacked by whites received inadequate protection, the Negroes formed a self-defense group called the Deacons for Defense and Justice.

As late as the second week of August there had been few disturbances outside the South. But on the evening of August 11, as Los Angeles sweltered in a heat wave, a highway patrolman halted a young Negro driver for speeding. The young man appeared intoxicated, and the patrolman arrested him. As a crowd gathered, law-enforcement officers were called to the scene. A highway patrolman mistakenly struck a bystander with his billy club. A young Negro woman, who was accused of spitting on the police, was dragged into the middle of the street.

When the police departed, members of the crowd began hurling rocks at passing cars, beating white motorists, and overturning cars and setting them on fire. The police reacted hesitantly. Actions they did take further inflamed the people on the streets.

The following day the area was calm. Community leaders attempting to mediate between Negro residents and the police received little cooperation from municipal authorities. That evening the previous night's pattern of violence was repeated.

Not until almost thirty hours after the initial flare-up did window smashing, looting, and arson begin. Yet the police utilized only a small part of their forces.

Few police were on hand the next morning when huge crowds gathered in the business district of Watts, two miles from the location of the original disturbance, and began looting. In the absence of police response the looting became bolder and spread into other areas. Hundreds of women and children from five housing projects clustered in or near Watts took part. Around noon extensive fire-bombing began. Few white persons were attacked; the principal intent of the rioters now seemed to be to destroy property owned by whites, in order to drive white "exploiters" out of the ghetto.

The chief of police asked for the help of the National Guard, but the arrival of the military units was delayed for several hours. When the Guardsmen arrived, they, together with police, made heavy use of firearms. Reports of "sniper fire" increased. Several persons were killed by mistake. Many more were injured.

Thirty-six hours after the first Guard units arrived, the main force of the riot had been blunted. Almost four thousand persons were arrested. Thirty-four were killed and hundreds injured. Approximately 35 million dollars in damage had been inflicted.

The Los Angeles riot, the worst in the United States since the Detroit riot of 1943, shocked all who had been confident that race relations were improving in the North, and evoked a new mood in Negro ghettos across the country.

1966 The events of 1966 made it appear that domestic turmoil had become part of the American scene.

In March a fight between several Negroes and Mexican Americans resulted in a new flare-up in Watts. In May, after

The destruction in Watts, 1965

a police officer accidentally shot and killed a Negro, demonstrations by Negro militants again increased tension in Los Angeles.

Evidence was accumulating that a major proportion of riot participants were youths. Increasing race pride, skepticism about their job prospects, and dissatisfaction with the inadequacy of their education caused unrest among students in Negro colleges and high schools throughout the country. Students and youths were the principal participants in at least six of the thirteen spring and early-summer disorders of 1966.

July 12, 1966, was a hot day in Chicago. Negro youngsters were playing in water gushing from an illegally opened fire hydrant. Two police officers, arriving on the scene, closed the hydrant. A Negro youth turned it on again, and the police officers arrested him. A crowd gathered. Police reinforcements arrived. As the crowd became unruly several Negro youths were arrested.

Rumors spread that the arrested youths had been beaten and that police were turning off fire hydrants in Negro neighborhoods but leaving them on in white areas. Sporadic window breaking, rock throwing, and fire-bombing lasted for several hours. Most of the participants were teen-agers.

In Chicago, as in other cities, the long-standing grievances of the Negro community needed only minor incidents to trigger violence.

On the evening of July 13, the day after the fire-hydrant incident, rock throwing, looting, and fire-bombing began again. For several days thereafter the pattern of violence was repeated. Police responding to calls were subjected to random gunfire. Rumors spread. The press talked in highly exaggerated terms of "guerrilla warfare" and "sniper fire."

Before the police and 4200 National Guardsmen managed

The National Guard in Cleveland, 1966

to restore order, scores of civilians and police had been injured. There were 533 arrests, including 155 juveniles. Three Negroes were killed by stray bullets, among them a thirteen-year-old boy and a pregnant fourteen-year-old girl.

Less than a week later Ohio National Guardsmen were mobilized to deal with an outbreak of rioting that continued for four nights in the Hough section of Cleveland. It is probable that Negro extremists, although they neither instigated nor organized the disorder, exploited and enlarged it. Amidst widespread reports of "sniper fire," four Negroes, including one young woman, were killed; many others, several young children among them, were injured. Law-enforcement officers were responsible for two of the deaths, a white man firing from a car for a third, and a group of young white vigilantes for the fourth.

Some news media keeping "tally sheets" of the disturbances began to apply the term *riot* to acts of vandalism and relatively minor disorders.

At the end of July the National States Rights Party, a white extremist organization that advocates deporting Negroes and other minorities, preached racial hatred at a series of rallies in Baltimore. Bands of white youths were incited into chasing and beating Negroes. A court order halted the rallies.

Forty-three disorders and riots were reported during 1966. Although there were considerable variations in circumstances, intensity, and length, they were usually ignited by a minor incident fueled by antagonism between the Negro population and the police.

Spring 1967 In the spring of 1967 disorders broke out at three Southern Negro universities at which SNCC (Student Nonviolent Coordinating Committee), a militant antiwhite organization, had been attempting to organize the students.

On Friday, April 7, learning that Stokely Carmichael was speaking at two primarily Negro universities (Fisk, and Tennessee Agricultural and Industrial) in Nashville, and receiving information that some persons were preparing to riot, the police adopted an emergency riot plan.

On the following day Carmichael and others, including South Carolina Senator Strom Thurmond, spoke at a symposium at Vanderbilt University in Nashville.

That evening the Negro operator of a restaurant located near Fisk University summoned police to arrest an allegedly intoxicated Negro soldier.

Within a few minutes students, many of them members of SNCC, began to picket the restaurant. A squad of riot police arrived and soon became the focus of attention. Spectators gathered. When a city bus was halted and attacked by members of the crowd, a Negro police lieutenant fired five shots into the air.

Rocks and bottles were thrown and additional police were called into the area. Officers fired a number of shots over the heads of the crowd. The students and spectators gradually dispersed.

On the following evening, after negotiations between students and police broke down, crowds again began forming. Police fired over their heads, and shots were fired back at the police. On the fringes of the campus several white youths aimed shots at a police patrol wagon.

A few days later, when police raided the home of several young Negro militants, they confiscated a half-dozen bottles prepared as Molotov cocktails.

About a month later students at Jackson State College, in Jackson, Mississippi, were standing around after a political rally when two Negro police officers pursued a speeding car, driven by a Negro student, onto the campus. When the officers tried to arrest the driver, the students interfered. The police called for reinforcements. A crowd of several hundred persons quickly gathered, and some rocks were thrown.

On the following evening an even larger crowd assembled. When police attempted to disperse it by gunfire, three persons were hit. One of them, a young Negro, died the next day. The National Guard restored order.

Six days later, on May 16, two separate Negro protests were taking place in Houston. One group was picketing a garbage dump in a Negro residential neighborhood where a Negro child had drowned. Another was demonstrating at a junior high school, on the grounds that Negro students were disciplined more harshly than white.

That evening college students who had participated in the protests returned to the campus of Texas Southern University. About 50 of them were grouped around a twenty-one-year-old student, D.W., a Vietnam veteran, who was seeking to stimulate further protest action. A dispute broke out, and D.W. reportedly slapped another student. When the student threatened D.W., he left, armed himself with a pistol, and returned.

In response to the report of a disturbance two unmarked police cars with four officers arrived. Two of the officers questioned D.W., discovered he was armed with a pistol, and arrested him.

When, a short time later, one of the police cars returned to the campus, it was met by rocks and bottles thrown by students. As police called for reinforcements sporadic gunshots reportedly came from the men's dormitory. The police returned the fire.

For several hours gunfire punctuated unsuccessful attempts by community leaders to negotiate a truce between the students and the police.

When several tar barrels were set afire in the street and shooting broke out again, police decided to enter the dormitory. A patrolman, struck by a ricocheting bullet, was killed. After clearing all 480 occupants from the building, police searched it and found one shotgun and two .22 caliber pistols. The origin of the shot that killed the officer was not determined.

As the summer of 1967 approached, Americans, conditioned by three years of reports of riots, expected violence. But they had no answers to hard questions:

    What was causing the turmoil?
    Was the violence organized? If so, by whom?
    Was there a pattern to the disorders?

Detroit: A Profile of Violence

The full Report contains profiles of a selection of the disorders that took place during the summer of 1967. The cities studied include Tampa, Florida; Cincinnati, Ohio; Atlanta, Georgia; four suburban communities of northern New Jersey and the New Jersey cities of Newark, Plainfield, and New Brunswick (where a riot threatened but failed to materialize); and Detroit, Michigan.

These "riot profiles" answer some of the questions about how the disorders happened, who participated in them, and how local officials, police forces, and the National Guard responded.

An illustrative excerpt follows.

At 3:45 A.M. on Sunday, July 22, the Detroit Police Department raided the last of five "blind pigs" on its list. The blind pigs had had their origin in prohibition days and survived as private social clubs. They were often after-hours drinking and gambling spots. The last to be raided was located at the corner of Twelfth Street and Clairmount.

On Twelfth Street, with its high incidence of vice and crime, the issue of police brutality was a recurrent theme. About a month before the raid of the blind pig on Twelfth Street, Danny Thomas was murdered. He was twenty-seven, a Negro Army veteran, and he was killed by a gang of white youths. His murder inflamed the community.

A banner story in the *Michigan Chronicle*, the city's Negro newspaper, began: "As James Meredith marched again Sunday to prove a Negro could walk in Mississippi without fear, a young woman who saw her husband killed by a white gang shouting, 'Niggers keep out of Rouge Park,' lost her baby. Relatives were upset that the full story of the murder was not being told, apparently in an effort to prevent the incident from sparking a riot."

Some Negroes believed that the daily newspapers' treatment of the story was further evidence of a double standard: playing up crimes by Negroes, playing down crimes committed against Negroes.

The Thomas family lived only four or five blocks from the blind pig on Twelfth Street.

On either side of Twelfth Street were neat, middle-class districts. Along Twelfth Street itself, however, overcrowded apartment houses created a density of more than twenty-one thousand persons per square mile, almost double the city average.

The movement of people, when the slums of "Black Bottom" had been cleared for urban renewal, had changed Twelfth Street from an integrated community into an almost totally black one in which only a number of merchants remained white. Only 18 per cent of the residents were homeowners. Twenty-five per cent of the housing was considered so substandard as to require clearance. Another 19 per cent had many deficiencies.

The crime rate was almost double that of the city as a whole. A Detroit police officer told Commission investigators that prostitution was so widespread that officers made arrests only when soliciting became blatant. The proportion of broken families was more than twice that in the rest of the city.

The Twelfth Street area had been determined to be a community of high stress and tension in a survey conducted by Dr. Ernest Harburg of the University of Michigan. An overwhelming majority of the residents indicated dissatisfaction with their environment. Ninety-three per cent said that they wanted to move out of the neighborhood. Seventy-three per cent felt that the streets were not safe. Ninety-one per cent believed that a person was likely to be robbed or beaten

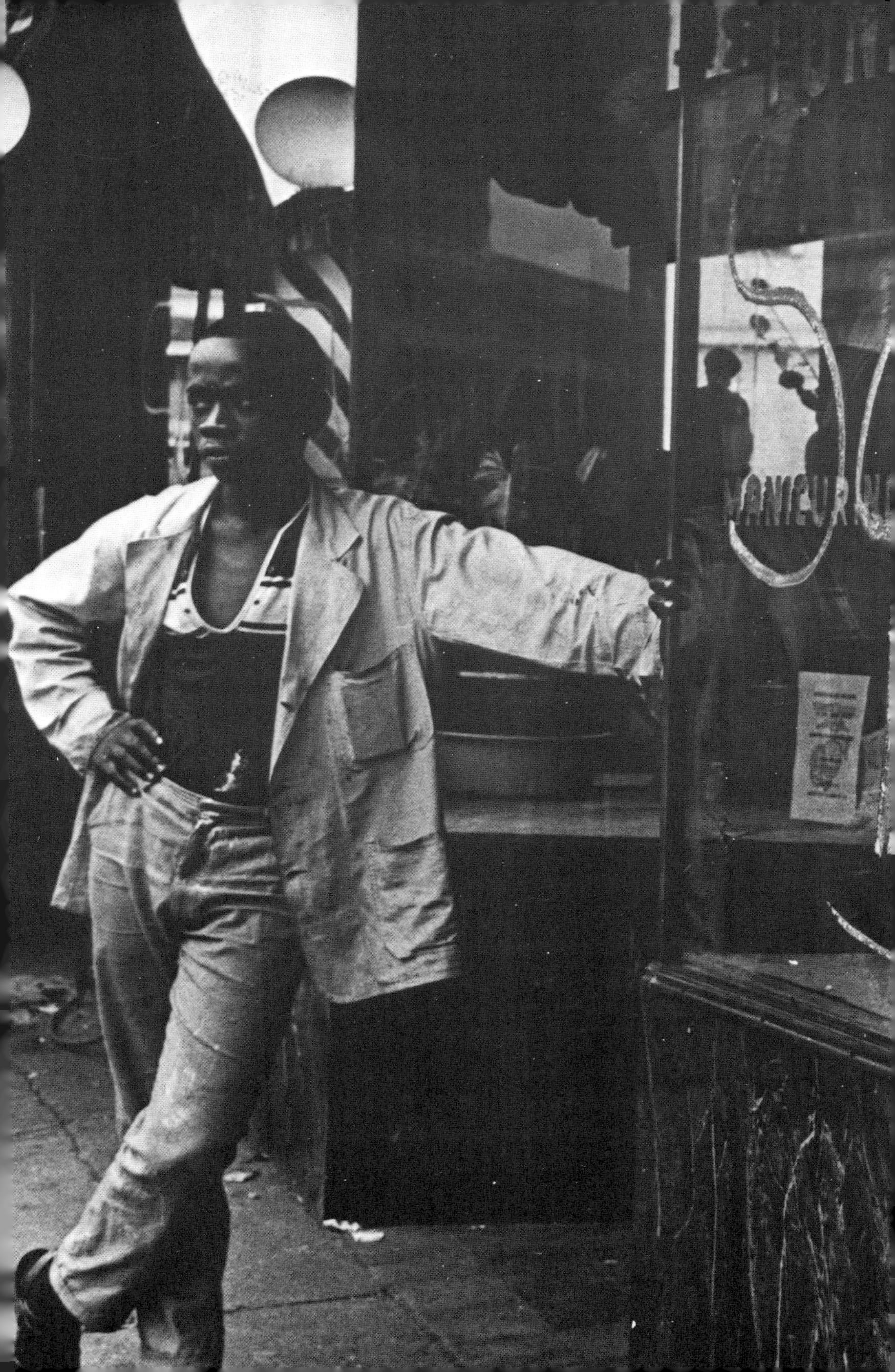

at night. Fifty-eight per cent knew of a fight within the last twelve months in which a weapon had been employed. Thirty-two per cent stated that they themselves owned a weapon. Fifty-seven per cent were worried about fires.

As for municipal services, a significant proportion of those living in the area of Twelfth Street felt them to be inferior: Thirty-six per cent were dissatisfied with the schools, 43 per cent with the city's contribution to the neighborhood, 77 per cent with the recreational facilities, and 78 per cent believed police did not respond promptly when they were summoned for help.

The city of Detroit was losing population. Its prosperous middle-class whites were moving to the suburbs and being replaced by unskilled Negro migrants. Between 1960 and 1967 the Negro population rose from just under 30 per cent to an estimated 40 per cent of the total.

In a decade, the school system had gained 50,000 to 60,000 children. Fifty-one per cent of the elementary school classes were overcrowded. The system needed 1650 more teachers and 1000 additional classrooms, at a combined cost of 63 million dollars, simply to achieve the state-wide average.

Of 300,000 school children, 171,000, or 57 per cent, were Negro. According to the Detroit Superintendent of Schools, twenty-five different school districts surrounding the city spent up to $500 more per pupil per year than Detroit. In the inner-city schools, more than half the pupils who entered high school became dropouts.

Detroit's strong union structure had created excellent conditions for most working men, but civil service and government workers were comparatively disadvantaged and dissatisfied. The "Blue Flu" had struck the city in June as police officers, forbidden to strike, had staged a sick-out. In September the teachers were to go on strike. The starting wages for a plumber's helper were almost equal to the salary of a police officer or teacher.

Some unions, traditionally closed to Negroes, zealously guarded training opportunities. In January of 1967 the school system notified six apprenticeship trades that it would not open new apprenticeship classes unless a large number of Negroes were included. In the fall of the year some of the programs were still closed.

High school diplomas from inner-city schools were regarded by personnel directors as less than valid. Unemployment was at a five-year peak in July and in the Twelfth Street area was estimated to be between 12 and 15 per cent for Negro men and 30 per cent or higher for those under twenty-five years of age.

The more education a Negro had, the greater the disparity between his income and that of a white with the same level of education. The income of whites and Negroes with a seventh-grade education was about equal. The median income of whites with a high school diploma was $1600 more per year than that of Negroes. White college graduates made $2600 more than Negro graduates. In fact, so far as income was concerned, it made very little difference to a Negro man whether he had attended school for eight years or twelve. A study conducted in the fall of 1967 at Northwestern High School in the inner city showed that although 50 per cent of the dropouts had found work, 90 per cent of the 1967 graduating class was unemployed.

Mayor Jerome Cavanagh had appointed many Negroes to key positions in his administration. In elective offices, however, the Negro population was still underrepresented. Of nine councilmen, one was a Negro. Of seven school-board members, two were Negroes.

Federal programs had brought nearly 360 million dollars

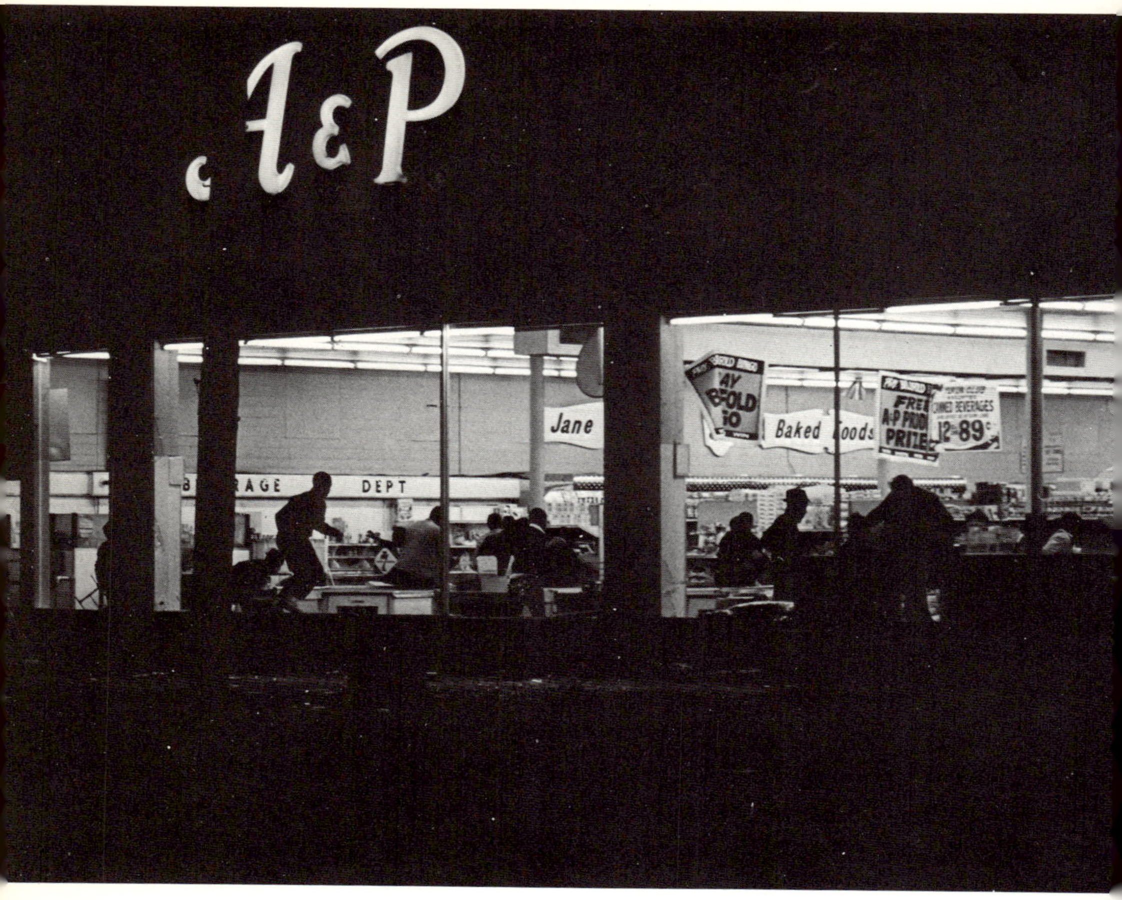
A&P
Jane
DEPT

to the city between 1962 and 1967, but the money appeared to have had little impact at the grass roots. Urban renewal, for which 38 million dollars had been allocated, was opposed by many residents of the poverty area.

Because of its financial straits the city was unable to produce on promises to correct such conditions as poor garbage collection and bad street lighting, a failure which brought constant complaints from Negro residents.

Police expected to find about two dozen patrons when they raided the blind pig on Twelfth Street shortly after 3 A.M. Sunday. That night, however, it was the scene of a party for several servicemen, two of whom were back from Vietnam. Instead of two dozen patrons, police found eighty-two. Some voiced resentment at the police intrusion.

An hour went by before all eighty-two could be transported from the scene. Before long a crowd of about two hundred had gathered. A few minutes after 5:00 A.M., just after the last of those arrested had been hauled away, an empty bottle smashed through the rear window of a police car. A litter basket smashed through the window of a store. Rumors circulated of excess force used by the police during the raid. A youth, whom police nicknamed "Mr. Greensleeves" because of the color of his shirt, was shouting: "We're going to have a riot!" and exhorting the crowd to vandalism.

At 5:20 A.M. Commissioner of Police Ray Girardin was notified. He immediately called Mayor Cavanagh. Seventeen officers from other areas were ordered into the tenth precinct. By 6:00 A.M. police strength had grown to 369 men. Of these, however, only 43 were committed to the immediate riot area. By that time the number of persons on Twelfth Street was growing into the thousands and widespread window smashing and looting had begun.

By 7:50 A.M., when a seventeen-man commando unit

attempted to make the first sweep to clear the area, an estimated three thousand persons were on Twelfth Street. As the sweep moved down the street, the people gave way to one side and then flowed back behind it.

A shoe-store manager said he waited vainly for police for two hours as the store was being looted. At 8:25 A.M. someone in the crowd yelled, "The cops are coming!" The first flames of the riot billowed from the store. Firemen who responded were not harassed. The flames were extinguished.

Approximately a fourth of the police department, more than a thousand men, had reported for duty by midmorning. More than half of these were in or near the six-block riot area. About a hundred officers were attempting to establish a cordon. There was, however, no interference with looters and police were refraining from the use of force. Commissioner Girardin said: "If we had started shooting in there not one of our policemen would have come out alive. I am convinced it would have turned into a race riot in the conventional sense."

A police officer in the riot area told Commission investigators that neither he nor his fellow officers were instructed as to what they were supposed to be doing. Witnesses tell of officers standing behind sawhorses as an area was being looted—and still standing there much later when the mob had moved elsewhere.

At one point a rumor threaded through the crowd that a man had been bayoneted by the police. The crowd became belligerent. At approximately 1:00 P.M. Sunday, numerous officers reported injuries from rocks, bottles, and other objects thrown at them. Smoke billowed from four fires, the first reported since the fire at the shoe store early in the morning. Firemen became targets for rocks and bottles when they answered the alarms.

Mayor Cavanagh met with community and political leaders

at police headquarters at 2 P.M. Until then there had been hope that as people blew off steam the riot would dissipate. Now the opinion was nearly unanimous that additional forces would be needed. A request was made for state police aid. An hour later 360 officers were assembling at the armory.

At that time looting was spreading from the Twelfth Street area to other main thoroughfares. A spirit of carefree nihilism was taking hold. To riot and destroy appeared more and more to become ends in themselves. Late Sunday afternoon it appeared to one observer that the young people were "dancing amidst the flames."

A Negro plain-clothes officer was standing at an intersection when a man threw a Molotov cocktail into a business establishment at the corner. In the heat of the afternoon, fanned by the twenty- to twenty-five mile per hour winds of both Sunday and Monday, the fire reached the home next door within minutes. As residents uselessly sprayed the flames with garden hoses, the fire jumped from roof to roof of adjacent two- and three-story buildings. Within the hour the entire block was in flames. The ninth house in the burning row belonged to the arsonist who had thrown the Molotov cocktail.

Residents of some areas organized rifle squads to protect fire fighters. Elsewhere, especially as the wind-whipped flames began to overwhelm the Detroit Fire Department and more and more residences burned, the firemen were subjected to curses and rock throwing.

The Detroit Fire Department is, on a per capita basis, one of the smallest in the nation—because of a lack of funds. The department had no mutual aid agreement with surrounding communities and could not quickly call in reinforcements from outlying areas. It was almost nine o'clock Sunday evening before the first help arrived.

As the afternoon progressed, the fire department's radio

carried repeated messages of apprehension and orders of caution:

> If you have trouble at all, pull out! Protect yourselves! Proceed away from the scene. . . . All companies without police protection—all companies without police protection—orders are to withdraw. Do not try to put out the fires!

It was 4:30 P.M. when the firemen, some of them exhausted by the heat, abandoned an area of approximately one hundred square blocks on either side of Twelfth Street to await protection from police and National Guardsmen. During the course of the riot firemen were to withdraw on 250 occasions.

At 4:20 P.M. Mayor Cavanagh requested that the National Guard be brought into Detroit. The first troops were on the streets by seven that evening. At 7:45 P.M. the mayor issued a proclamation instituting a 9 P.M. to 5 A.M. curfew. At 9:15 P.M. a sixteen-year-old boy, superficially wounded while looting, became the first reported gunshot victim. Before dawn a white woman, a white youth, and five looters had been shot, one of them accidentally, while struggling with a police officer. A Negro youth and a National Guardsman were injured by gunshots of undetermined origin. A private guard shot himself while pulling his revolver from his pocket.

During the daylight hours on Monday, nine more persons were killed by gunshots. Included among those critically injured when they were accidentally trapped in the line of fire were an eight-year-old Negro girl and a fourteen-year-old white boy.

At 2:15 A.M. Monday, Michigan's Governor George Romney and Mayor Cavanagh had decided to ask for Federal assistance. Shortly before noon the President of the United States authorized the sending of a task force of paratroopers, and later that afternoon the first Federal troops arrived at

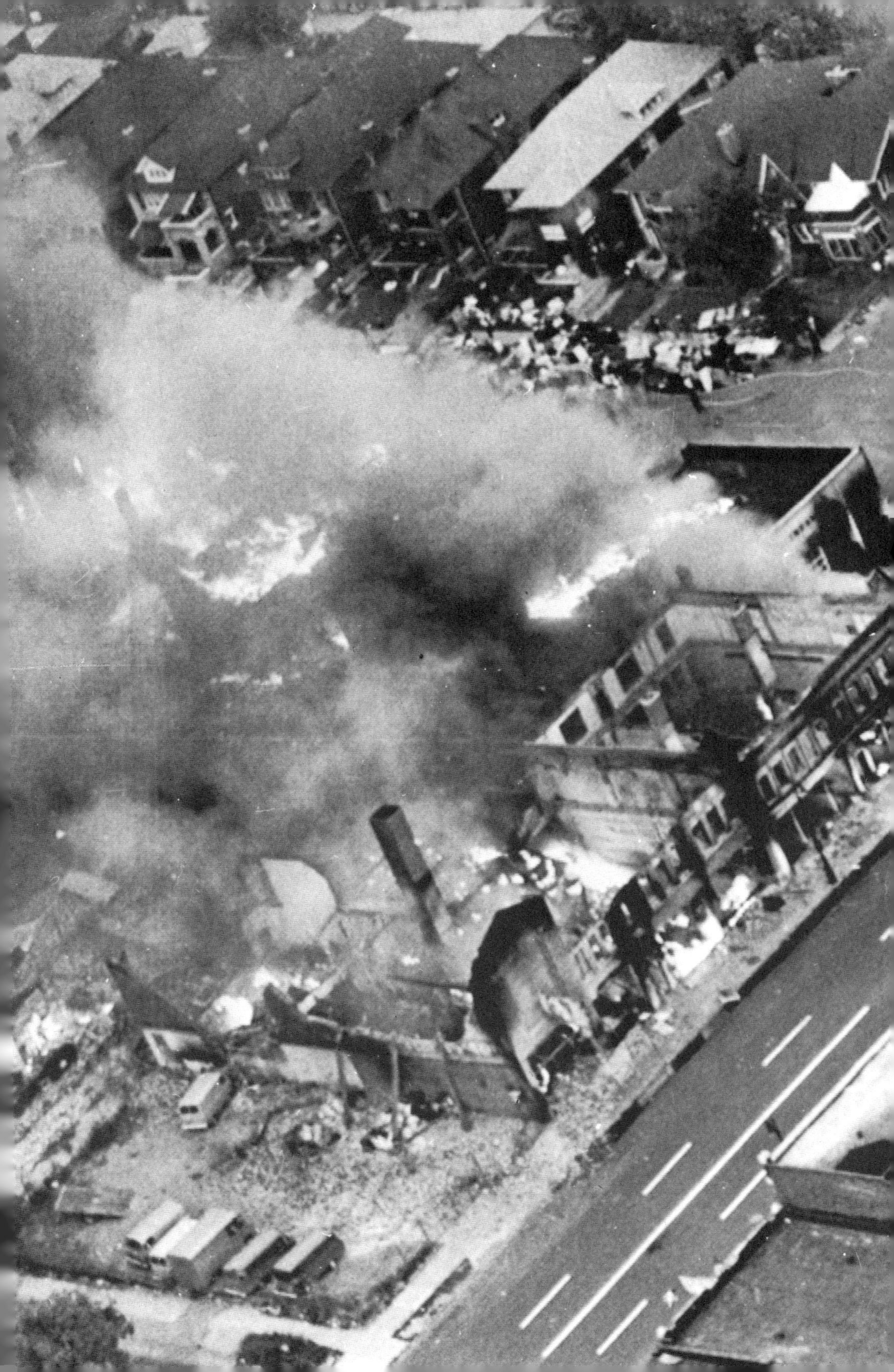

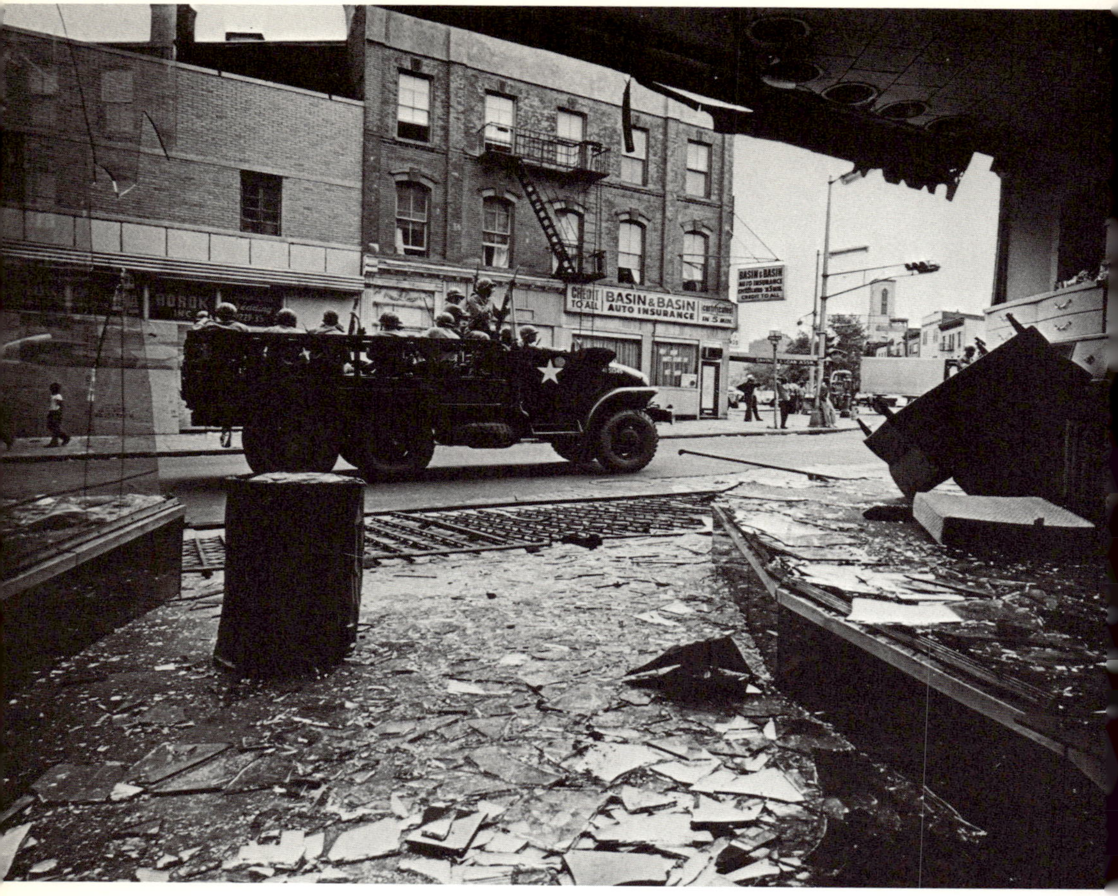
BASIN & BASIN
CREDIT
TO ALL
BASIN & BASIN
AUTO INSURANCE

Selfridge Air Force Base near the city. It was toward midnight on Monday that the President signed a proclamation federalizing the Michigan National Guard and authorizing the use of the paratroopers.

At that time there were nearly five thousand Guardsmen in the city. Fatigue, lack of training, and the haste with which they had had to be deployed reduced their effectiveness during the riot. Some of them had traveled two hundred miles and then were on duty for thirty hours straight. Some had never received riot training. They were given on-the-spot instructions on mob control—only to discover that there were no mobs and that the situation they faced on the darkened streets was one for which they were unprepared.

It appeared that Guardsmen had not been warned regarding the danger of overreaction and the necessity of great restraint in using weapons. The young troopers could not be expected to know that their lack of fire discipline made them a danger not only to the civilian population but to themselves.

A Detroit newspaper reporter who spent a night riding in a command jeep told a Commission investigator of machine guns being fired accidentally, street lights being shot out by rifle fire, and buildings being placed under siege on the sketchiest reports of sniping. Troopers would fire, and immediately from the distance there would be answering fire, sometimes consisting of tracer bullets.

In one instance, the newsman related, a report was received on the jeep radio that an Army bus was pinned down by sniper fire at an intersection. National Guardsmen and police, arriving from various directions, jumped out and began asking each other: "Where's the sniper fire coming from?" As one Guardsman pointed to a building everyone rushed about, taking cover. A soldier, alighting from a jeep, accidentally pulled the trigger on his rifle. As the shot reverberated through the darkness an officer yelled: "What's going on?" "I don't know," came the answer. "Sniper, I guess."

Late Monday evening, a half dozen civilians and one National Guardsman were wounded by shots of undetermined origin. Shortly before midnight five young Negro men, riding in a station wagon, saw a jeep sitting at the curb. Believing it to be a road block, they slowed down. Simultaneously a shot rang out; a National Guardsman was hit in the ankle. Other National Guardsmen at the scene thought the shot had come from the station wagon. They fired at least seventeen shots into it. All the occupants were injured, one fatally.

At about the same time firemen, police, and National Guardsmen at an intersection two blocks away came under fire from what they believed were rooftop snipers to the southeast. They responded with a hail of fire. When the shooting ceased, a young firefighter lay dead.

Before dawn on Tuesday paratroopers comprising Army Task Force Detroit moved into the city from the air-force base. At this time, according to Lieutenant General John L. Throckmorton and Colonel A. R. Bolling of the Task Force, the city was saturated with fear. The National Guardsmen were afraid, the residents were afraid, and the police were afraid. Numerous persons, the majority of them Negroes, were being injured by gunshots of undetermined origin.

With persons of every description arming themselves, and with guns being fired accidentally or on the vaguest pretext all over the city, it became more and more impossible to tell who was shooting at whom. Some firemen had begun to carry guns. One accidentally shot and wounded a fellow fireman. Another injured himself.

At approximately midnight on Tuesday a machine gunner on a tank was startled by several shots and asked where they had come from. The assistant gunner pointed toward a flash in the window of an apartment house. The machine gunner opened fire. Twenty-one-year-old Valerie Hood had her arm nearly severed by the slugs that ripped through the apartment walls. Her four-year-old niece, Tonya Blanding, fell dead. A few seconds earlier Bill Hood, nineteen, had lighted a cigarette while standing at the apartment window.

On Wednesday R.R., a white absentee owner of an expensive three-story house on L Street, arrived from New York to evict tenants with whom he had been having trouble. On the advice of his attorney he took his seventeen-year-old brother and another youth with him as witnesses while he changed the locks during the absence of the tenants. For protection they brought a .22 caliber rifle with them. When R.R. refused to admit the tenants upon their return, they threatened to obtain the help of the National Guard.

The National Guard claims that at approximately the same time it received information to the effect that several men had evicted the legal occupants of the house and intended to start sniping after dark.

A National Guard column of approximately thirty men surrounded the house at dusk. A tank was stationed on a lawn across the street. The captain in charge set off an explosive device similar to a firecracker to attract the attention of the occupants, then ordered them to come out. He heard two shots of undetermined origin and saw a "fire streak" coming from an upstairs window. He thereupon gave the order to fire.

As hundreds of shots poured into the first- and second-story windows and ricocheted off the walls, the three young men inside fled to the third floor and hid in a closet, protected by a large chimney. They were finally able to wave an item of clothing out a window as a sign of surrender. The firing from rifles and machine guns had been so intense that a pair of stone columns was shot nearly in half and an estimated $10,000 worth of damage was inflicted in a period of a few minutes.

The young men were arrested as snipers. They were among the hundreds of arrestees brought into the tenth precinct station, to become the victims of officers who took it upon themselves to carry on investigations and extract confessions. Dozens of charges of police brutality emanated from the station as prisoners were brought in uninjured and later had to be taken to a hospital.

Citing the sniper danger, officers throughout the department had taken off their badges. They also had taped over the license plates and the numbers of the police cars. Identification of individual officers became virtually impossible.

On a number of occasions officers fired at fleeing looters and then made little attempt to determine whether their shots had hit anyone. Later some of the persons were discovered dead or injured in the streets.

In one such case police and National Guardsmen were interrogating a youth suspected of arson when, according to officers, he attempted to escape. As he vaulted over the hood of an automobile, an officer fired his shotgun. The youth disappeared on the other side of the car. Without making an investigation, the officers and Guardsmen returned to their car and drove off.

Not until a Detroit newspaper editor presented to the police the statements of several witnesses claiming that the youth had been shot by police after he had been told to run did the department launch an investigation. Not until three weeks after the shooting did an officer come forward to identify himself as the one who had fired the fatal shot. The

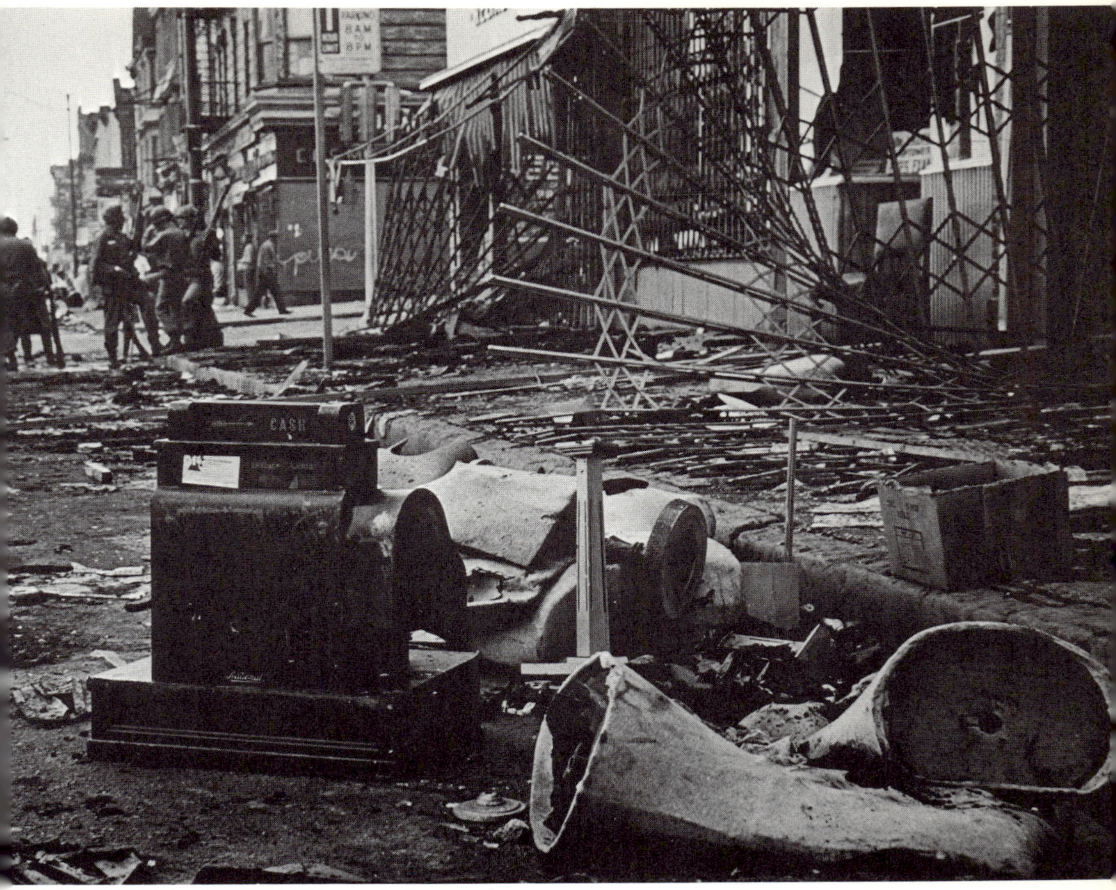
CASH

Detroit prosecutor's office, citing conflicts in the testimony of the score of witnesses, declined to press charges.

The looting and fire bombing of the riot had virtually ceased by late Tuesday, although there were hundreds of reports of incidents—mostly reports of sniper fire—from seven until eleven that night. During the daylight hours on Wednesday and until late that night, there were 789 such reports.

From the time of their arrival in the city, General Throckmorton and his staff felt that the major task of the troops was to reduce fear and restore an air of normalcy. In order to accomplish this, every effort was made to establish contact and rapport between the troops and the residents. Troopers, 20 per cent of whom were Negro, began helping to clean up the streets, collect garbage, and trace persons who had disappeared in the confusion. Residents in the neighborhoods responded with soup and sandwiches for the troops. In areas where the National Guard tried to establish rapport with the citizens a similar response was reported.

Within hours after the arrival of the paratroops, the area occupied by them was the quietest in the city, bearing out General Throckmorton's view that the key to quelling disorder is to saturate an area with "calm, determined, and hardened professional soldiers." Loaded weapons, he believes, are unnecessary. Troopers had strict orders not to fire unless they could see the specific person at whom they were aiming. Mass fire was forbidden.

During five days in the city, 2700 Army troops expended only 201 rounds of ammunition, almost all during the first few hours—after which even stricter fire discipline was enforced. General Throckmorton ordered the weapons of all military personnel unloaded, but either the order failed to reach many National Guardsmen or else it was disobeyed.

Of the forty-three persons who were killed during the riot, thirty-three were Negro and ten were white. Action by police officers accounted for twenty and, very likely, twenty-one of the deaths. Action by the National Guard accounted for seven and, very likely, nine. Action by the Army was responsible for one. Two deaths were the result of action by store owners. Four persons died accidentally. Rioters were responsible for two, and perhaps three, of the deaths, a private guard for one. A white man is suspected of murdering a Negro youth. The perpetrator of one of the killings remains unknown.

In all, more than 7200 persons were arrested. By midnight Monday 4000 were incarcerated in makeshift jails. Some were kept as long as thirty hours on buses. Others spent days in an underground garage without toilet facilities. An uncounted number were people who had merely been unfortunate enough to be on the wrong street at the wrong time. Included were members of the press whose attempts to show their credentials had been ignored.

By Thursday, July 27, most riot activity had ended. The paratroopers were removed from the city on Saturday. On Tuesday, August 1, the curfew was lifted and the National Guard moved out.

What makes people angry enough, frustrated enough, despairing enough, to riot?

Although specific grievances varied from city to city, at least twelve deeply held grievances can be identified and ranked into three levels of relative intensity.

> First level of intensity:
> Police practices
> Unemployment and underemployment

Inadequate housing

Second level of intensity:
Inadequate education
Poor recreation facilities and programs
Ineffectiveness of the political structure and grievance mechanisms

Third level of intensity:
Disrespectful white attitudes
Discriminatory administration of justice
Inadequacy of Federal programs
Inadequacy of municipal services
Discriminatory consumer and credit practices
Inadequate welfare programs

The President directed the Commission to investigate "to what extent, if any, there has been planning or organization in any of the riots."

To carry out this part of the President's charge, the Commission established a special investigative staff supplementing the field teams that made the general examination of the riots in twenty-three cities. The unit examined the data collected by Federal agencies and Congressional committees, including thousands of documents supplied by the Federal Bureau of Investigation; gathered and evaluated information from local and state law-enforcement agencies and officials; and conducted its own field investigation in selected cities.

On the basis of all the information collected, the Commission concludes that:

The urban disorders of the summer of 1967 were not caused by, nor were they the consequence of, any organized plan or "conspiracy."

Specifically, the Commission has found no evidence that all or any of the disorders or the incidents that led to them were planned or directed by any organization or group, international, national, or local.

Militant organizations, local and national, and individual agitators, who repeatedly forecast and called for violence, were active in the spring and summer of 1967. We believe that they sought to encourage violence, and that they helped to create an atmosphere that contributed to the outbreak of disorder.

We recognize that the continuation of disorder and the polarization of the races would provide fertile ground for organized exploitation in the future.

Search for a Pattern

The "typical" riot of recent years is sometimes seen as a massive uprising against white people, involving widespread burning, looting, and sniping, either by all ghetto Negroes or by an uneducated, Southern-born Negro underclass of habitual criminals or "riffraff." Often identified as the primary spark of violence is one of the following: an agitator at a protest demonstration; the coverage of events by the news media; or an isolated "triggering" or "precipitating" incident. The pattern of violence is sometimes said to consist of a uniform set of stages involving a succession of confrontations and withdrawals by two cohesive groups—the police on one side and a riotous mob on the other. Often it is assumed that there is no effort within the Negro community to reduce the violence. Sometimes the only remedy prescribed is application of the largest possible police or control force, as early as possible.

What we have found does not validate these conceptions.

We have been unable to identify constant patterns in all aspects of civil disorders. We have found that disorders are unusual, irregular, complex, and in the present state of knowledge, unpredictable social processes. As is true of many human events, civil disorders do not unfold in orderly sequences.

We have examined the 1967 disorders within a few months after their occurrence and under pressing time limitations. While we have collected information of considerable immediacy, analysis will undoubtedly improve with the passage and perspective of time and with the further accumulation and refinement of data.

However, on the basis of information derived from our surveys we offer the following generalizations:

58 WHAT HAPPENED?

No civil disorder was "typical" in all respects. Viewed in a national framework, the disorders of 1967 varied greatly in terms of violence and damage. While a relatively small number were major under our criteria, and a somewhat larger number were serious, most of the disorders would have received little or no national attention as "riots" had the nation not been sensitized by the more serious outbreaks.

While the civil disorders of 1967 were racial in character, they were not *inter*racial. The 1967 disorders, as well as earlier disorders of the recent period involved action within Negro neighborhoods against symbols of white American society—authority and property—rather than against white persons.

Despite extremist rhetoric, there was no attempt to subvert the social order of the United States. Instead, most of those who attacked white authority and property seemed to be demanding fuller participation in the social order and the material benefits enjoyed by the vast majority of American citizens.

Disorder did not typically erupt as a result of a single "triggering" or "precipitating" incident. Instead, it developed out of an increasingly disturbed social atmosphere, in which, typically, a series of tension-heightening incidents over a period of weeks or months became linked in the minds of many in the Negro community with a shared reservoir of underlying grievances.

There was, typically, a complex relationship between the series of tension-heightening incidents and the underlying grievances. For example, grievances about allegedly abusive police practices were often aggravated in the minds of many Negroes by incidents involving the police, or the inaction of municipal authorities on Negro complaints about police action. When grievance-related incidents recurred and rising tensions were not satisfactorily resolved, a cumulative process took place: Prior incidents were

Counterrioters urging looters to "cool it"

A trivial incident like an illegally opened fire hydrant can ignite tension into violence.

readily recalled and grievances were reinforced. At some point in this process a further incident—in itself often routine or even trivial—became the breaking point, and tension spilled over into violence.

Many grievances in the Negro community result from the discrimination, prejudice, and powerlessness which Negroes often experience. They also result from the severely disadvantaged social and economic conditions of many Negroes as compared with those of whites in the same city and, more particularly, in the predominantly white suburbs.

Characteristically, the typical rioter was not a hoodlum, habitual criminal, or riffraff; nor was he a recent migrant, a member of an uneducated underclass, or a person lacking broad social and political concerns. Instead, he was a teen-ager or young adult, a lifelong resident of the city in which he rioted, a high-school dropout—but somewhat better educated than his Negro neighbor. And almost invariably he had a menial job or was underemployed: i.e., he earned less than $3000 a year from either part-time or full-time work, or had dropped out of the labor force and did not seek work. He was proud of his race, extremely hostile to both whites and middle-class Negroes, and, though informed about politics, highly distrustful of the political system and of political leaders.

Numerous Negro counterrioters walked the streets urging rioters to "cool it." The typical counterrioter resembled in many respects the majority of Negroes, who neither rioted nor took action against the rioters; that is, the noninvolved. But certain differences are crucial: The counterrioter was better educated and had a higher income than either the rioter or the noninvolved.

Negotiations between Negroes and white officials occurred during virtually all the disorders surveyed. The negotiations often involved young, militant Negroes as well as older, established leaders. Despite a setting of chaos and disorder, negotiations in many cases involved discussion of underlying grievances as well as the handling of the disorder by control authorities.

The chain we have identified—discrimination, prejudice, disadvantaged conditions, intense and pervasive grievances, a series of tension-heightening incidents, all culminating in the eruption of disorder at the hands of youthful, politically-aware activists—must be understood as describing the central trend in the disorders, not as an explanation of all aspects of the riots or of all rioters.

Some rioters, for example, may have shared neither the conditions nor the grievances of their Negro neighbors. Some may have coolly and deliberately exploited the chaos created by others. Some may have been drawn into the melee merely because they identified with, or wished to emulate, others. Nor do we intend to suggest that the majority of the rioters, who shared the adverse conditions and grievances, necessarily articulated in their own minds the connection between that background and their actions.

The background of disorder in the riot cities was typically characterized by severely disadvantaged conditions for Negroes, especially as compared with those for whites; a local government often unresponsive to these conditions; Federal programs which had not yet reached a significantly large proportion of those in need; and the resulting reservoir of pervasive and deep grievance and frustration in the ghetto.

In the immediate aftermath of disorder, the *status quo* of daily life before the disorder generally was quickly restored. Yet despite some notable public and private efforts, little basic change took place in the conditions underlying the disorder. In some cases, the result was increased distrust between blacks and whites, diminished interracial communication, and growth of Negro and white extremist groups.

PART II: WHY DID IT HAPPEN?

The Basic Causes

We have seen what happened. Why did it happen? What factors within the society at large created a mood for violence among so many urban Negroes in the summer of 1967?

The record before this Commission reveals that the causes of recent racial disorders are imbedded in a massive tangle of issues and circumstances—social, economic, political, and psychological—which arise out of the historical pattern of Negro–white relations in America.

These factors are both complex and interacting, but despite these complexities, certain fundamental matters are clear. Of these, the most fundamental is the racial attitude and behavior of white Americans toward black Americans. Race prejudice has shaped our history decisively in the past; it now threatens to do so again.

White racism is essentially responsible for the explosive mixture which has been accumulating in our cities since the end of World War II. At the base of this mixture are three of the most bitter fruits of white racial attitudes.

The first of these bitter fruits is surely the continuing exclusion of great numbers of Negroes from the benefits of economic progress through discrimination in employment and education, and the enforced confinement of Negroes in segregated housing and schools. The corrosive and degrading effects of this condition, and of the attitudes that underlie it, are the source of the deepest bitterness. They lie at the center of the problem of racial disorder.

The second source of bitterness is the massive and growing concentration of impoverished Negroes in our major cities. This is the result of Negro migration from the rural South and of the rapid Negro population growth. It is also the result of the continuing movement of the white middle class to the suburbs. The consequence of this concentration of impoverished people in our cities is a greatly increased burden on the already depleted resources of the cities which creates a growing crisis of deteriorating facilities and services and of unmet needs.

Third, in the teeming racial ghettos, segregation and poverty have combined to destroy opportunity and hope and to enforce failure. The ghettos too often mean men and women without jobs; families without men; and schools where children are processed instead of educated, until they return to the street—to crime, to narcotics, to dependency on welfare, and to bitterness and resentment against society in general and white society in particular.

These three forces—discrimination and segregation, the movement of Negroes to (and whites away from) the city, and the lack of opportunity that characterizes ghetto life—have converged on the inner city in recent years and on the people who live there.

At the same time, most whites and many Negroes outside the ghetto have prospered to a degree unparalleled in the history of civilization. Through television (as popular in the ghetto as anywhere else) and through other media of mass communication, American affluence has been endlessly flaunted before the eyes of the Negro poor and the jobless ghetto youth.

As Americans, most Negro citizens carry within themselves two basic aspirations of our society. They seek to share in both the material resources of our system and in its intangible benefits—dignity, respect, and acceptance. Outside the ghetto, many Negroes have succeeded in achieving a decent standard of life and in developing the inner resources which give life meaning and direction. Within the ghetto, however, it is rare that either aspiration is achieved.

Yet these facts alone, fundamental as they are, cannot be

DRY CLEANING
310
TAILOR
GAS RANGES
NEW & REBUILT
SALES-SERVICE-PARTS
Coca
SALES-

The climate of white violence: a bombed Negro church in Birmingham (top); the Ku Klux Klan on the march

said to have caused the disorders. Other and more immediate factors help explain why these events happened now.

The expectations aroused by the great judicial and legislative victories of the civil-rights movement have led to frustration, hostility, and cynicism because of the persistent gap between promise and fulfillment. The dramatic struggle for equal rights in the South has made Northern Negroes more sharply aware of their own economic inequalities, as reflected in the deprivations of ghetto life.

A climate that approves and encourages violence as a form of protest has been created by white terrorism directed against nonviolent protest. There have been instances of abuse and even of murder of civil-rights workers in the South. State and local officials have also resorted to violence in resisting desegregation in open defiance of law and Federal authority. And there have been some protest groups engaged in civil disobedience who have turned their backs on nonviolence, gone beyond the Constitutionally protected rights of petition and free assembly, and resorted to violence in an attempt to compel alteration of laws and policies with which they disagree.

This climate, one that tends to approve violence, is encouraged by 1) a general erosion of respect for authority in American society; 2) the reduced effectiveness of social standards and community restraints on violence and crime. These in turn have largely resulted from rapid urbanization and the dramatic reduction in the average age of the total population.

Finally, many Negroes have come to believe that they are being exploited politically and economically by the white "power structure." Negroes, like people in poverty everywhere, in fact lack the channels of communication, influence, and appeal that traditionally have been available to ethnic minorities within the city. In an earlier era, ethnic minorities—unburdened by color—were able to scale the walls of the white ghettos. But the frustrations of powerlessness among black Americans have led some of them to the conviction that there is no effective alternative to violence as a means of expression and redress, as a way of "moving the system." More generally the Negro's feeling of powerlessness has resulted in his alienation from and hostility toward the institutions of law and government, and the white society which controls the institutions. This is expressed in the reach toward racial consciousness and solidarity reflected in the slogan "Black Power."

These facts have combined to inspire a new mood among Negroes, particularly among the young. Self-esteem and enhanced racial pride are replacing apathy and submission to "the system." Moreover, the Negro youth, who make up over half the ghetto population, share the growing sense of alienation felt by many white youths in our country. Thus, their role in recent civil disorders reflects more than a shared sense of deprivation, and of victimization by white society; it must also be considered as part of the rising incidence of disruptive conduct engaged in by a segment of American youth throughout the society.

These conditions have created a volatile mixture of attitudes and beliefs which needs only a spark to ignite mass violence.

Strident appeals to violence, first heard from white racists, were echoed and reinforced in the summer of 1967 in the inflammatory rhetoric of black racists and militants. Throughout the year, extremists crisscrossed the country preaching a doctrine of Black Power and violence. Their rhetoric was widely reported in the mass media; it was echoed by local "militants" and organizations; it became the ugly background noise of the violent summer.

We cannot measure with any precision the influence in

The climate of black violence: Militants preach Black Power, racism and disorder.

NO
PARKING
8 AM TO 6 PM
MON. THRU FRI.
ARMY & NAVY
SALES STORE
MILITARY SUPPLIES
WINES
LIQUORS
SIMON'S
ARMY & NAVY
SALES STORE
BATTERY
PAWNBROKER
LOANS

the ghetto of these organizations and individuals, but we think it clear that the intolerable and unconscionable encouragement of violence heightened tensions, created a mood of acceptance and an expectation of violence, and thus contributed to the eruption of the disorders in the summer of 1967.

It is the convergence of all these factors that makes the role of the police so difficult and so significant.

Almost invariably the incident that ignites disorder arises from police action. Harlem, Watts, Newark, and Detroit—all the major outbursts of recent years—were precipitated by arrests by white police of Negroes for minor offenses.

But the police are not merely the spark. In the discharge of their obligation to maintain order and insure public safety in the disruptive conditions of ghetto life, they are inevitably involved in sharper and more frequent conflicts with ghetto residents than with the residents of other areas. Thus, to many Negroes, police have come to symbolize white power, white racism, and white repression.

And the fact is that many police do reflect and express these white attitudes. The atmosphere of hostility and cynicism in the ghetto is reinforced by a widespread perception among Negroes of the existence of police brutality and corruption, and of a "double standard" of justice and protection —one for Negroes and one for whites.

To this point, we have attempted only to identify the prime components of the "explosive mixture." In the sections that follow we seek to analyze these components in the perspective of history. Their meaning, however, is already clear:

In the summer of 1967 we have seen in our cities a chain reaction of racial violence. If we are heedless, none of us shall escape the consequences.

The Negro in America: A Historical Sketch

The events of the summer of 1967 are in large part the culmination of three hundred years of racial prejudice. Most Americans know little of the origins of the racial schism separating our white and Negro citizens. Few appreciate how central the problem of the Negro has been in our social policy. Fewer still understand that today's problems can be solved only if white Americans comprehend the rigid social, economic, and educational barriers that have prevented Negroes from participating in the mainstream of American life.

Only a handful of white Americans realize that Negro accommodation to the patterns of prejudice in American culture has been but one side of the coin. As slaves and as free men, Negroes have protested against oppression, and they have persistently sought equality in American society.

What follows is neither a history of the Negro in the

United States nor a full account of Negro protest movements. Rather, it is a brief narrative of a few historical events that illustrate the facts of rejection and the forms of protest. Here we call on history not to justify, but to help explain, for black and white Americans, a state of mind.

Twenty years after Columbus reached the New World, African Negroes, transported by Spanish, Dutch, and Portuguese traders, were arriving in the Caribbean Islands. Almost all came as slaves. By 1600 there were more than half a million slaves in the Western Hemisphere.

In Colonial America the first Negroes landed at Jamestown in August 1619. Within forty years Negroes had become a group apart, separated from the rest of the population by custom and law. Treated as servants for life, forbidden to intermarry with whites, deprived of their African traditions, and dispersed among Southern plantations, American Negroes lost tribal, regional, and family ties.

Through massive importation, their numbers increased rapidly. By 1776 some 500,000 Negroes were held in slavery and indentured servitude in the United States. Nearly one of every six persons in the country was a slave.

Americans disapproved a preliminary draft of the Declaration of Independence that indicted the King of England for waging

> cruel war against human nature itself, violating its most sacred rights of life and liberty in the persons of a distant people who never offended him, captivating and carrying them into slavery in another hemisphere, or to incur miserable death in their transportation thither.

Instead, Americans approved a document that proclaimed that "all men are created equal." The statement was an ideal, a promise. But it excluded the Negroes who were held in bondage, as well as the few who were free men.

The conditions in which Negroes lived had already led to protest. Racial violence was present almost from the beginning of the American experience. Throughout the eighteenth century, the danger of Negro revolts obsessed many white Americans. Slave plots of considerable scope were uncovered in New York in 1712 and 1714 and they resulted in bloodshed. Both whites and Negroes were slain.

Negroes were at first barred from serving in the Revolutionary Army. Recruiting officers were ordered in July 1775 to enlist no "stroller, Negro, or vagabond." Yet Negroes were already actively involved in the struggle for independence. Crispus Attucks, a Boston Negro, was perhaps the first American to die for freedom (on March 5, 1770, in an encounter with British sailors). Negroes had already fought in battles at Lexington and Concord. They were among the soldiers at Bunker Hill.

Fearing that Negroes would enlist in the British Army, which welcomed them, and facing a man-power shortage, the Continental Army accepted free Negroes in 1775. Slaves joined the British, and according to an estimate by Thomas Jefferson, more than thirty thousand Virginia slaves ran away in 1778 alone, presumably to enlist.

The individual states were enrolling both free and slave Negroes, and finally Congress authorized military service for slaves in 1778. They were to be emancipated in return for their service. By the end of the war, about five thousand Negroes had been in the ranks of the Continental Army. Those who had been slaves became free. But the liberty and equality implicit in American independence had meaning rather than application to them.

Massachusetts abolished slavery in 1783, and Connecticut, Rhode Island, New Jersey, Pennsylvania, and New York soon provided for gradual liberation. But relatively few Negroes lived in these states. The bulk of the Negro population was in the South, where white Americans had fortunes invested in slaves.

Although the Congress banned slavery in the Northwest Territory, delegates at the Constitutional Convention compromised with the institution of slavery in the following ways: 1) a slave counted as only three-fifths of a person for determining the number of representatives from a state to Congress; 2) Congress was prohibited from restricting the slave trade until after 1808; and 3) the free states were required to return fugitive slaves to their Southern owners.

Growing numbers of slaves in the South became permanently fastened in bondage, and slavery spread into the new Southern regions. When more slaves were needed for the cotton and sugar plantations in the Southwest, they were ordered from the "Negro-raising" states of the Old South or, despite Congressional prohibition of the slave trade, imported from Africa.

The laws of bondage became even more institutionalized. Masters retained absolute authority over their Negroes, who were unable to leave their masters' properties without written permission. Any white person, even those who owned no slaves—and they outnumbered slaveholders six to one— could challenge a truant slave and turn him over to a public official. Slaves could own no property, could enter into no contract, not even a contract of marriage, and had no right to assemble in public unless a white person was present. They had no standing in the courts.

The situation was hardly better for free Negroes. A few achieved material success, several owned slaves themselves, but the vast majority knew only poverty and suffered the indignity of rejection by white society. Forbidden to settle in some areas, segregated in others, they were targets of prejudice and discrimination.

In the South, free Negroes were denied freedom of movement, severely restricted in their choice of occupation, and forbidden to associate with whites or with slaves. They lived in constant danger of being enslaved. Whites could challenge their freedom, and an infraction of the law could put them into bondage. In both North and South, they were regularly victims of mobs. In 1829, for example, white residents invaded Cincinnati's "Little Africa," killed Negroes, burned their property, and ultimately drove half the black population from the city.

Some Americans, Washington and Jefferson among them, advocated the gradual emancipation of slaves. In the 1800s, a movement to abolish slavery grew in importance and strength. A few white abolitionist leaders wanted full equality for Negroes, but others sought only to eliminate the institution of slavery itself. And some antislavery societies, fearing that Negro members would unnecessarily offend those who were not in sympathy with abolitionist principles, denied membership to Negro abolitionists.

Most Americans were, in fact, against abolishing slavery. They refused to rent their halls for antislavery meetings. They harassed abolitionist leaders who sought to educate white and Negro children together. They attacked those involved in the movement. Mobs sometimes killed abolitionists and destroyed their property.

A large body of literature came into existence to prove that the Negro was imperfectly developed in mind and body; that he belonged to a lower order of man; that slavery was right on ethnic, economic, and social grounds. And the Scriptures were quoted in support of these contentions.

The institution of slavery spread rapidly during the first part of the nineteenth century. Less than one million Negroes were enslaved in 1800, but almost four million were slaves by 1860. Although some few white Americans had freed their slaves, most increased their holdings, for the invention of the cotton gin had made the cotton industry profitable. By mid-century, slavery in the South was a systematic and aggressive way of treating a whole race of people.

The despair of Negroes was evident. Malingering and sabotage tormented every slaveholder. The problem of runaway slaves was endemic. Some slaves—Gabriel Prosser in 1800, Denmark Vesey in 1822, Nat Turner in 1831, and others—turned to violence, and the sporadic uprisings that flared demonstrated a deep protest against a demeaning way of life.

Negroes who had material resources expressed their distress in other ways.

Paul Cuffee, Negro philanthropist and owner of a fleet of

THE NEGRO'S COMPLAINT

Forc'd from home and all its pleasures,
    Afric's coast I left forlorn;
To increase a stranger's treasures,
    O'er the raging billows borne.
Men from England bought and sold me,
    Paid my price in paltry gold;
But though slave they have enroll'd me,
    Minds are never to be sold.

Still in thought as free as ever—
    What are England's rights (I ask)
Me from my delights to sever,
    Me to torture, me to task?
Fleecy locks and black complexion
    Cannot forfeit Nature's claim;
Skins may differ, but affection,
    Dwells in White and Black the same.

Part of a broadside published by the American Anti-slavery Office in 1835. The seven-stanza poem was by John Greenleaf Whittier.

ships, transported, in 1816, a group of Negroes to a new home in Sierra Leone.

Forty years later, Martin R. Delany, Negro editor and physician, urged Negroes to settle elsewhere.

Equality of treatment for Negroes and their acceptance by the society at large were myths. Negro protest during the first half of the nineteenth century took the form of rhetoric, spoken and written. The protest combined denunciation of undemocratic oppression with pleas to the conscience of white America for the redress of grievances and the recognition of the Negro's Constitutional rights.

A few Negroes joined those white Americans who believed that only Negro emigration to Africa would solve racial problems. But most Negroes equated that program with banishment and felt themselves "entitled to participate in the blessings" of America.

The National Negro Convention Movement, formed in 1830, held conferences to publicize on a national scale the evils of slavery and the indignities heaped on free Negroes.

The American Moral Reform Society, founded by Negroes in 1834, rejected racial separatism and advocated uplifting "the whole human race, without distinction as to . . . complexion."

Other Negro reformers pressed for stronger racial consciousness and solidarity as the means to overcome racial barriers. Many took direct action to help slaves escape through the underground railroad. A few resisted discrimination by political action, even though most Negroes were barred from voting.

Frustration, disillusionment, anger, and fantasy marked the Negro's protest against the place in American society assigned to him. "I was free," Harriet Tubman said, "but there was no one to welcome me in the land of freedom. I was a stranger in a strange land."

When Frederick Douglass, the distinguished Negro abolitionist, addressed the citizens of Rochester on Independence Day, 1852, he told them:

> The Fourth of July is *yours,* not mine. *You* may rejoice, *I* must mourn. To drag a man into the grand illuminated temple of liberty, and call upon him to join you in joyous anthems, were inhuman mockery and sacrilegious irony. . . . Fellow citizens, above your national tumultuous joy, I hear the mournful wail of millions, whose chains, heavy and grievous yesterday, are today rendered more intolerable by the jubilant shouts that reach them. . . .

The 1850s brought Negroes increasing despair as the problem of slavery was debated by the nation's leaders. The Compromise of 1850, which restricted slavery to the south of 36 degrees, 30 minutes of north latitude, settled no basic issue. Neither did the Kansas-Nebraska Act of 1854, which repealed the Compromise, opened northern territory to slavery, and set the stage for a battle between the pioneer farmers and the slaveholders for possession of Kansas. Despair deepened near the end of the decade when a Supreme Court decision, written by Chief Justice Taney in 1857, declared that Dred Scott, a slave, could not bring suit in a Federal court because he was not and could never be a citizen, since Negroes, within the meaning and intent of the Constitution, were deemed inferior persons and not "citizens."

But the abolitionist movement was growing. *Uncle Tom's Cabin* appeared in 1852 and sold more than 300,000 copies that year. Soon presented on the stage throughout the North, it dramatized the cruelty of slave masters and overseers and condemned a culture based on human degradation and exploitation. The election of Abraham Lincoln to the presidency on an antislavery platform gave hope that the end of slavery was near.

Frederick Douglass

An illustration from Uncle Tom's Cabin *by Harriet Beecher Stowe*

But by the time Lincoln took office, seven Southern states had seceded from the Union, and four more soon joined them.

The Civil War and Emancipation renewed Negro faith in the vision of a racially egalitarian and integrated American society. But Americans, after having been roused by wartime crisis, would again fail to destroy what abolitionists had described as the "sins of caste."

Negroes volunteered for military service during the Civil War—the struggle, as they saw it, between the slave states and the free states. They were rejected.

Not until a shortage of troops plagued the Union Army in 1862 were segregated units of "United States Colored Troops" formed. Not until 1864 did these men receive the same pay as white soldiers. A total of 186,000 Negroes served.

The Emancipation Proclamation of 1863 freed few slaves at first, but it had immediate significance as a symbol. Negroes could hope again for equality.

But there were, at the same time, bitter signs of racial unrest. Violent rioting occurred in Cincinnati in 1862, when Negro and Irish hands competed for work on the river boats. Lesser riots took place in Newark, New Jersey, and in Buffalo and Troy, New York, the result of combined hostility to the war and fear that Negroes would take white jobs.

The most violent of the troubles took place in the New York City Draft Riots in July 1863, when white workers, mainly Irish-born, embarked on a three-day rampage.

In an article, "New York's Bloodiest Week" (published in *American Heritage*, June 1959) Lawrence Lader describes the mood and motivations of New York's Irish immigrants at that time:

> Desperately poor and lacking real roots in the community, they had the most to lose from the draft. Further, they were

A newspaper cartoon of the day reflects the Negro's response to the Emancipation Proclamation.

CUTTING HIS OLD ASSOCIATES
Man of Color: "Ugh! Get out. I ain't one ob you no more. I'se a Man, I is."

bitterly afraid that even cheaper Negro labor would flood the North if slavery ceased to exist.

All the frustrations and prejudices the Irish had suffered were brought to a boiling point. . . . At pitiful wages they had slaved on the railroads and canals, had been herded into the most menial jobs as carters and stevedores. . . . Their crumbling frame tenements . . . were the worst slums in the city.

Their first target was the office of the provost-marshal in charge of conscription. Seven hundred people quickly ransacked the building and set it on fire. The crowd refused to permit firemen into the area, and the whole block was gutted. Then the mob spilled into the Negro area, where many were slain and thousands forced to flee town. The police were helpless until Federal troops arrived on the third day and restored control.

Union victory in the Civil War promised the Negroes freedom but hardly equality or immunity from white aggression. Scarcely was the war ended when racial violence erupted in New Orleans. Negroes proceeding to an assembly hall to discuss the franchise were charged by police and special troops. These routed the Negroes with guns, bricks, and stones, killed some at once, and pursued and killed others who were trying to escape.

Federal troops restored order. But thirty-four Negroes and four whites were reported dead and over two hundred people were injured. General Sheridan later said:

> At least nine-tenths of the casualties were perpetrated by the police and citizens by stabbing and smashing in the heads of many who had already been wounded or killed by policemen . . . it was not just a riot but an absolute massacre by the police . . . a murder which the mayor and police . . . perpetrated without the shadow of necessity.

A newspaper drawing of August 1, 1863, picturing the New York City Draft Riots

Reconstruction was a time of hope, the period when the Thirteenth, Fourteenth, and Fifteenth Amendments were adopted, giving Negroes the vote and the promise of equality.

But campaigns of violence and intimidation accompanied these optimistic expressions of a new age. The Ku Klux Klan and other secret organizations sought to suppress the emergence into society of the new Negro citizens. Major riots occurred in Memphis, Tennessee, where forty-six Negroes were reported killed and seventy-five wounded, and in the Louisiana centers of Colfax and Coushatta, where more than a hundred Negro and white Republicans were massacred.

Nevertheless, in 1875 Congress enacted the first significant civil-rights law. It gave Negroes the right to equal accommodations, facilities, and advantages of public transportation, inns, theaters, and places of public amusement. But the law had no effective enforcement provisions and was, in fact, poorly enforced. Although bills to provide Federal aid to education for Negroes were prepared, none passed, and educational opportunities remained meager.

But Negroes were elected to every Southern legislature, twenty served in the United States House of Representatives, two represented Mississippi in the United States Senate, and a prominent Negro politician was Governor of Louisiana for forty days.

Opposition to Negroes in state and local government was always open and bitter. In the press and on the platform they were described as ignorant and depraved. Critics made no distinction between Negroes who had graduated from Dartmouth and those who had graduated from the cotton fields. Every available means was employed to drive Negroes from public life. Negroes who voted or held office were refused jobs or punished by the Ku Klux Klan. One group in Mississippi boasted of having killed 116 Negroes and thrown their bodies into the Tallahatchie River. In a single South Carolina county six men were murdered and more than 300 whipped during the first six months of 1870.

The Federal government seemed helpless. Having withdrawn the occupation troops as soon as the Southern states organized governments, the President was reluctant to send them back. In 1870 and 1871, after the Fifteenth Amendment was ratified, Congress enacted several laws to protect the right of citizens to vote. They were seldom enforced, and the Supreme Court struck down most of the important provisions in 1875 and 1876.

As Southern white governments returned to power, beginning with Virginia in 1869 and ending with Louisiana in 1877, the program of relegating the Negro to a subordinate place in American life was accelerated.

Disfranchisement was the first step. Negroes who defied the Klan and tried to vote faced an array of deceptions and obstacles: Polling places were changed at the last minute, without notice to Negroes; severe time limitations were imposed on marking complicated ballots; and votes cast incorrectly in a maze of ballot boxes were nullified. The suffrage provisions of state constitutions were rewritten to disfranchise Negroes who could not read, understand, or interpret the Constitution. Some state constitutions permitted those who failed the tests to vote—if their ancestors had been eligible to vote on January 1, 1860, when no Negro could vote anywhere in the South.

In 1896 Negroes registered in Louisiana totalled 130,344. In 1900, after the state rewrote the suffrage provisions of its constitution, Negroes on the registration books numbered only 5320. Essentially the same thing happened in the other states of the former Confederacy.

When the Supreme Court, in 1883, declared the Civil

Rights Act of 1875 unconstitutional, Southern states began to enact laws to segregate the races.

In 1896 the Supreme Court in *Plessy v. Ferguson* approved "separate but equal" facilities; it was then that segregation became an established fact, by law and by custom. Negroes and whites were separated on public carriers and in all places of public accommodation, including hospitals and churches. In courthouses, whites and Negroes took oaths on separate Bibles. In most communities, whites were separated from Negroes in cemeteries.

Segregation invariably meant discrimination. On trains all Negroes, including those holding first-class tickets, were allotted a few seats in the baggage car. Negroes in public buildings had to use freight elevators and toilet facilities reserved for janitors. Schools for Negro children were at best a weak imitation of those for whites, as states spent ten times more to educate white youngsters than Negroes. Discrimination in wages became the rule, whether between Negro and white teachers of similar training and experience, or between common laborers on the same job.

Some Northern states enacted civil-rights laws in the 1880s, but Negroes in fact were treated little differently in the North from in the South.

As Negroes moved north in substantial numbers toward the end of the century they discovered that equality of treatment was only a dream in Massachusetts, New York, or Illinois. They were crowded by local ordinances into one section of the city, where housing and public services were generally substandard. Overt discrimination in employment was a general practice. Employment opportunities apart from menial tasks were few. Most labor unions excluded Negroes from membership, or granted membership in separate and powerless Jim Crow locals.

The kind of work Negroes could expect to find when they moved north, shown in a cartoon of the early 1900's

THEIR SON IN THE CITY

Yet when Negroes secured employment during strikes, labor leaders castigated them for not understanding the principles of trade unionism. And when Negroes sought to move into the mainstream of community life by seeking membership in the organizations around them—educational, cultural, and religious—they were invariably rebuffed.

By the twentieth century, the Negro was at the bottom of American society. Disfranchised, Negroes throughout the country were excluded by employers and labor unions from white-collar jobs and skilled trades. Jim Crow laws and farm tenancy characterized Negro existence in the South. About 100 lynchings occurred every year in the 1880s and 1890s. There were 161 lynchings in 1892. As increasing numbers of Negroes migrated to Northern cities race riots became commonplace. Northern whites, even many former abolitionists, began to accept the white South's views on race relations.

That Northern whites would resort to violence was made clear in anti-Negro riots in New York, 1900; Springfield, Ohio, 1904; Greensburg, Indiana, 1906; and Springfield, Illinois, 1908.

The Springfield, Illinois, riot lasted three days. It was initiated by a white woman's charge of rape by a Negro, inflamed by newspapers, intensified by crowds of whites gathered around the jail demanding that the Negro, arrested and imprisoned, be lynched. When the sheriff transferred the accused and another Negro to a jail in a nearby town, rioters headed for the Negro section and attacked homes and businesses owned by or catering to Negroes. White owners who showed handkerchiefs in their windows averted harm to their stores. One Negro was summarily lynched; others were dragged from houses and streetcars and beaten. By the time National Guardsmen could reach the scene, six persons were dead—four whites and two Negroes. Property damage was extensive. Many Negroes left Springfield, hoping to find better conditions elsewhere, especially in Chicago.

Booker T. Washington was born in slavery and was still a child when the Civil War freed the Negroes. He was the principal of Tuskegee Normal and Industrial Institute in Alabama in 1885 when he delivered the Atlanta Exposition Address that made him famous. It was at this time that he articulated the much-quoted separate-but-equal doctrine: "In all things that are purely social we can be separate as the fingers, yet one as the hand in all things essential to human progress." From 1885 until his death in 1915, Washington was the most prominent Negro in America. Publicly he advocated a policy of accommodation, conciliation, and gradualism. Privately he spent thousands of dollars fighting disfranchisement and segregation laws.

Washington believed that by helping themselves, by creating and supporting their own businesses, by proving their usefulness to society through the acquisition of education, wealth, and morality, Negroes would earn the respect of the white man and thus eventually gain their Constitutional rights.

Self-help and self-respect appeared a practical and sure, if gradual, way of ultimately achieving racial equality. Washington's doctrines also gained support because they appealed to race pride: If Negroes believed in themselves, stood together, and supported each other, they would be able to shape their destinies.

In the early years of the century, a small group of Negroes, led by W.E.B. Du Bois, formed the Niagara Movement to oppose Washington's program. Washington had put economic progress before politics, had accepted the separate-but-equal theory, and had opposed agitation and protest.

Du Bois and his followers stressed political activity as the basis of the Negro's future, insisted on the inequity of Jim Crow laws, and advocated agitation and protest.

In sharp language, the Niagara group placed responsibility for the race problem squarely on the whites. The aims of the movement were voting rights and "the abolition of all caste distinctions based simply on race and color."

Although Booker T. Washington tried to crush his critics, Du Bois and the Negro "radicals," as they were called, enlisted the support of a small group of influential white liberals and socialists. Together, in 1909–10, they formed the National Association for the Advancement of Colored People.

The NAACP hammered at the walls of prejudice by organizing Negroes and well-disposed whites, by aiming propaganda at the whole nation, and by taking legal action in courts and legislatures.

Almost at the outset of its career, the NAACP prevailed upon the Supreme Court to declare unconstitutional two discriminatory statutes. In 1915 the Court struck down the Oklahoma "grandfather clause," a provision in several Southern state constitutions which, together with voting tests, had the effect of excluding from the vote those whose ancestors had been ineligible to vote in 1860. Two years later, the Supreme Court outlawed municipal residential segregation ordinances.

These NAACP victories were the first legal steps in a long fight against disfranchisement and segregation.

During the first quarter of the twentieth century, the Federal government enacted no new legislation to ensure equal rights or opportunities for Negroes and made little attempt to enforce existing laws despite flagrant violations of Negro civil rights.

In 1913 members of Congress from the South introduced

A commemorative postage stamp picturing Booker T. Washington

W. E. B. DuBois

bills to Federalize the Southern segregation policy. They wished to ban interracial marriages in the District of Columbia, segregate white and Negro Federal employees, and introduce Jim Crow laws in the public carriers of the District. The bills did not pass, but segregation practices were extended in Federal offices, shops, rest rooms, and lunchrooms.

The nation's capital became as segregated as any in the former Confederate states.

Elsewhere there was violence. In East St. Louis, Illinois, a riot in July 1917 claimed the lives of thirty-nine Negroes and nine whites, as a result of the fear of white working men that Negro advances in economic, political, and social status were threatening their own security and status.

When the labor force of an aluminum plant went on strike, the company hired Negro workers. A labor union delegation called on the mayor and asked that further migration of Negroes to East St. Louis be stopped. As the men were leaving the city hall they heard that a Negro had accidentally shot a white man during a holdup.

In a few minutes rumor had replaced fact; the shooting was said to have been intentional. It was also rumored that a white woman had been insulted and that two white girls had been shot. By this time, three thousand people had congregated and were crying for vengeance. Mobs roamed the streets, beating Negroes. Policemen did little more than take the injured to hospitals and disarm Negroes.

The National Guard restored order. When the governor withdrew the troops, tensions were still high, and scattered episodes broke the peace. The press continued to emphasize the incidence of Negro crimes. White pickets and Negro workers at the aluminum company skirmished, and on July

National Guardsmen escorting a Negro to safety in East St. Louis

some whites drove through the main Negro neighborhood firing into homes. Negro residents armed themselves. When a police car drove down the street, Negroes riddled it with gunshot.

The next day a Negro was shot on the main street and a new riot was under way. The authority on the event records that the area became a "bloody half mile" for three or four hours. Streetcars were stopped and Negroes, without regard to age or sex, were pulled off and stoned, clubbed, and kicked. Mob leaders calmly shot and killed Negroes who were lying in blood in the street. As the victims were placed in an ambulance the crowds cheered and applauded.

Other rioters set fire to Negro homes, and by midnight the Negro section was in flames and Negroes were fleeing the city. There were forty-eight dead, hundreds injured, and more than three hundred buildings destroyed.

When the United States entered World War I in 1917, the country again faced the question of whether American citizens should have the right to serve, on an equal basis, in defense of their country. More than two million Negroes registered under the Selective Service Act, and some 360,000 were called into service.

The Navy rejected Negroes except as menials. The Marine Corps rejected them altogether. The Army formed them into separate units, commanded, for the most part, by white officers. Only after enormous pressure did the Army permit Negro candidates to train as officers in a segregated camp. Mistreated at home and overseas, Negro combat units performed exceptionally well under French commanders, who refused to heed American warnings that Negroes were inferior people.

Negro soldiers returning home were mobbed for attempting to use facilities open to white soldiers. Of the seventy Negroes lynched during the first year after the war, a substantial number were soldiers. Some were lynched in uniform.

The Ku Klux Klan was reorganized in 1915 and was flourishing again by 1919. Its program for "uniting native-born white Christians for concerted action in the preservation of American institutions and the supremacy of the white race" was implemented by flogging, branding with acid, tarring and feathering, hanging, and burning. It destroyed the elemental rights of many Negroes—and of some whites.

Violence took the form of lynchings and riots, and major riots by whites against Negroes took place in 1917 in Chester, Pennsylvania, and Philadelphia; in 1919 in Washington, D.C., Omaha, Charleston, Longview, Texas, Chicago, and Knoxville; in 1921 in Tulsa.

The Chicago riot of 1919 flared from the increase in Negro population, which had more than doubled in ten years. Jobs were plentiful, but housing was not, and when black neighborhoods expanded into white sections of the city, trouble developed. Between July 1917 and March 1921, fifty-eight Negro houses were bombed and recreational areas were sites of racial conflict.

The riot itself started on Sunday, July 27, with stone throwing and sporadic fighting at adjoining white and Negro beaches. A Negro boy swimming off the Negro beach drifted into water reserved for whites and drowned. Young Negroes claimed he had been struck by stones and demanded the arrest of a white man. Instead, police arrested a Negro. Negroes attacked policemen. News spread throughout the city. White and Negro groups clashed in the streets, two persons died, and fifty were wounded.

On Monday, Negroes coming home from work were attacked. Later, when whites drove cars through Negro neighborhoods and fired weapons, Negroes retaliated. Twenty more were killed and hundreds wounded. On Tuesday, a handful more were dead, 129 injured. Rain began to fall. The mayor finally called in the state militia. After nearly a week of violence, the city quieted down.

In the period between the two World Wars the NAACP dominated the strategy of racial advancement. The NAACP drew its strength from large numbers of Southern Negroes who had migrated to Northern cities, and from a small but growing Negro group of professionals and businessmen. It projected the image of the "new Negro"—race-proud and self-reliant, believing in racial cooperation and self-help, and determined to fight for his Constitutional rights. This image was reflected in the work of writers and artists (known as the Harlem Renaissance) who drew upon the Negro's own cultural tradition and experience. W.E.B. Du Bois, editor of the *Crisis,* the NAACP publication, symbolized the new mood and exerted great influence.

The NAACP did extraordinary service, giving legal defense to victims of race riots and of unjust judicial proceedings. It obtained the release of the soldiers who had received life sentences on charges of rioting against intolerable conditions in Houston in 1917. It successfully defended Negro sharecroppers in Elaine, Arkansas, who in 1919 had banded together to gain fairer treatment. They had become the objects of a massive armed hunt by whites to put them "in their place," and were charged with insurrection when they resisted.

The NAACP secured the acquittal, with the help of Clarence Darrow, of Dr. Ossian Sweet and his family. The Sweets, who had moved into a white neighborhood in Detroit, shot at a mob attacking their home and killed a man. They were eventually judged to have committed the act in self-defense.

Less successful were attempts to prevent school segregation in Northern cities. Gerrymandering of school boundaries and other devices used by boards of education were fought with written petitions, verbal protests to school officials, legal suits, and in several cities, school boycotts. All proved of no avail.

The thrust of the NAACP was primarily political and legal, but the National Urban League, founded in 1911 by philanthropists and social workers, sought an economic solution to the Negroes' problems. Sympathetic with Booker T. Washington's point of view, believing in conciliation, gradualism, and moral suasion, the Urban League searched out industrial opportunities for Negro migrants to the cities, using arguments that appealed to the white businessman's sense of economic self-interest and also to his conscience.

Another important figure who espoused an economic program to ameliorate the Negroes' condition was A. Philip Randolph, an editor of the *Messenger*. He regarded the NAACP as a middle-class organization unconcerned about the Negro's economic problems. Taking a Marxist position on the causes of prejudice and discrimination, Randolph called for a new and radical Negro, unafraid to demand his rights as a member of the working class. He advocated physical resistance to white mobs, but he believed that only united action of black and white workers against capitalists would achieve social justice.

Although Randolph addressed himself to the urban working masses, few of them ever read the *Messenger*. The one man who reached the masses of frustrated and disillusioned migrants in the Northern ghettos was Marcus Garvey.

Garvey, who in 1914 founded the Universal Negro Improvement Association (UNIA), aimed to liberate both Africans and American Negroes from their oppressors. His utopian method was the wholesale migration of American Negroes to Africa. Contending that whites would always be racist, he stressed racial pride and history, denounced integration, and insisted that the black man develop "a distinct racial type of civilization of his own . . . and work out his salvation in his motherland."

On a more practical level he urged support of Negro businesses, and through the UNIA organized a chain of groceries, restaurants, laundries, a hotel, a printing plant, and a steamship line. When several prominent Negroes called the attention of the United States government to irregularities in the management of the steamship line, Garvey was jailed, then deported for having used the mails to defraud.

But Garvey dramatized, as no one before, the bitterness and alienation of the Negro slum dwellers who, having come North with great expectations, found only overcrowded and deteriorated housing, mass unemployment, and race riots.

Negro labor, relatively unorganized and the target of discrimination and hostility, was hardly prepared for the Depression of the 1930s. To a disproportionate extent, Negroes lost their jobs in cities and worked for starvation wages in rural areas. Although organizations such as the National Urban League tried to improve employment opportunities, 65 per cent of Negro employables were in need of public assistance by 1935.

Public assistance was given on a discriminatory basis, especially in the South. For a time, Dallas and Houston gave no relief at all to Negro families. In general, Negroes had more difficulty than whites in obtaining assistance, and their relief benefits were smaller. Some religious and charitable

Marcus Garvey

A bread line during the Depression

organizations excluded Negroes from their soup kitchens. The New Deal marked a turning point in American race relations.

Negroes found much in the New Deal to complain about. Discrimination existed in many agencies. Federal housing programs expanded urban ghettos. In the South money from the Agricultural Adjustment Administration went chiefly to white landowners, while crop restrictions forced many Negro sharecroppers off the land.

Nevertheless, Negroes shared in relief, jobs, and public housing, and Negro leaders, who felt the open sympathy of many highly placed New Dealers, held more prominent political positions than at any time since President Taft's administration. The creation of the Congress of Industrial Organizations (CIO), with its avowed philosophy of nondiscrimination, made the notion of an alliance of black and white workers something more than a visionary's dream.

The Depression, the New Deal, and the CIO reoriented Negro protest toward concern with economic problems. Negroes conducted "Don't Buy Where You Can't Work" campaigns in a number of cities, boycotted and picketed commercial establishments owned by whites, and sought equality in American society through an alliance with white labor.

The NAACP came under attack from some Negroes. Du Bois resigned as editor of the *Crisis* in 1934 because, believing in the value of collective racial economic endeavor, he saw little point in protesting disfranchisement and segregation without pursuing economic goals. Younger critics also disagreed with the NAACP's gradualism on economic issues.

Undeterred, the NAACP broadened the scope of its legal work. In some states voters were required to pay a certain amount of money, usually six months before an election, to be eligible to vote. The NAACP fought a vigorous though unsuccessful battle to outlaw this poll tax. An equally vigorous attack was made on the practice of denying Negroes the right to vote in the primary elections by which political parties nominated their candidates for office. The NAACP won this battle when the Supreme Court declared white primaries unconstitutional in 1944. But the heart of NAACP litigation was a long-range campaign against segregation and the most obvious inequities in the Southern school systems: the lack of professional and graduate schools, and the low salaries received by Negro teachers.

Not until about 1950 would the NAACP make a direct assault against school segregation on the legal ground that separate facilities were inherently unequal.

The Growth of a Movement

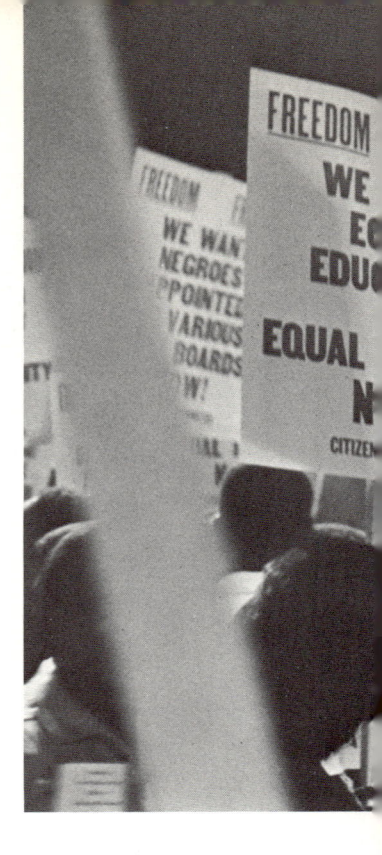

During World II Negroes learned again that fighting for their country brought them no nearer to full citizenship. Rejected when they tried to enlist, they were accepted into the Army according to the proportion of the Negro population to that of the country as a whole—but only in separate units, and those mostly noncombat. The United States thus fought racism in Europe with a segregated fighting force.

The Red Cross, with the government's approval, separated Negro and white blood in banks established for wounded servicemen—even though the blood banks were largely the work of a Negro physician, Charles Drew.

Not until 1949 would the Armed Forces begin to adopt a firm policy against segregation.

Negroes seeking employment in defense industries were embittered by policies like that of a West Coast aviation factory which declared openly that Negroes "will be considered only as janitors and in other similar capacities. . . . Regardless of their training as aircraft workers, we will not employ them."

Two new movements marked Negro protest: a threatened march on Washington, and the Congress of Racial Equality (CORE).

In 1941, consciously drawing on the power of the Negro vote and concerned with the economic problems of the urban slum dweller, A. Philip Randolph announced a mass Negro convergence on Washington unless President Roosevelt secured employment for Negroes in the defense industries. The President's Executive Order 8802, establishing a Federal Fair Employment Practices Commission, forestalled the demonstration. Even without enforcement powers, the FEPC set a precedent for treating fair employment practices as a civil right.

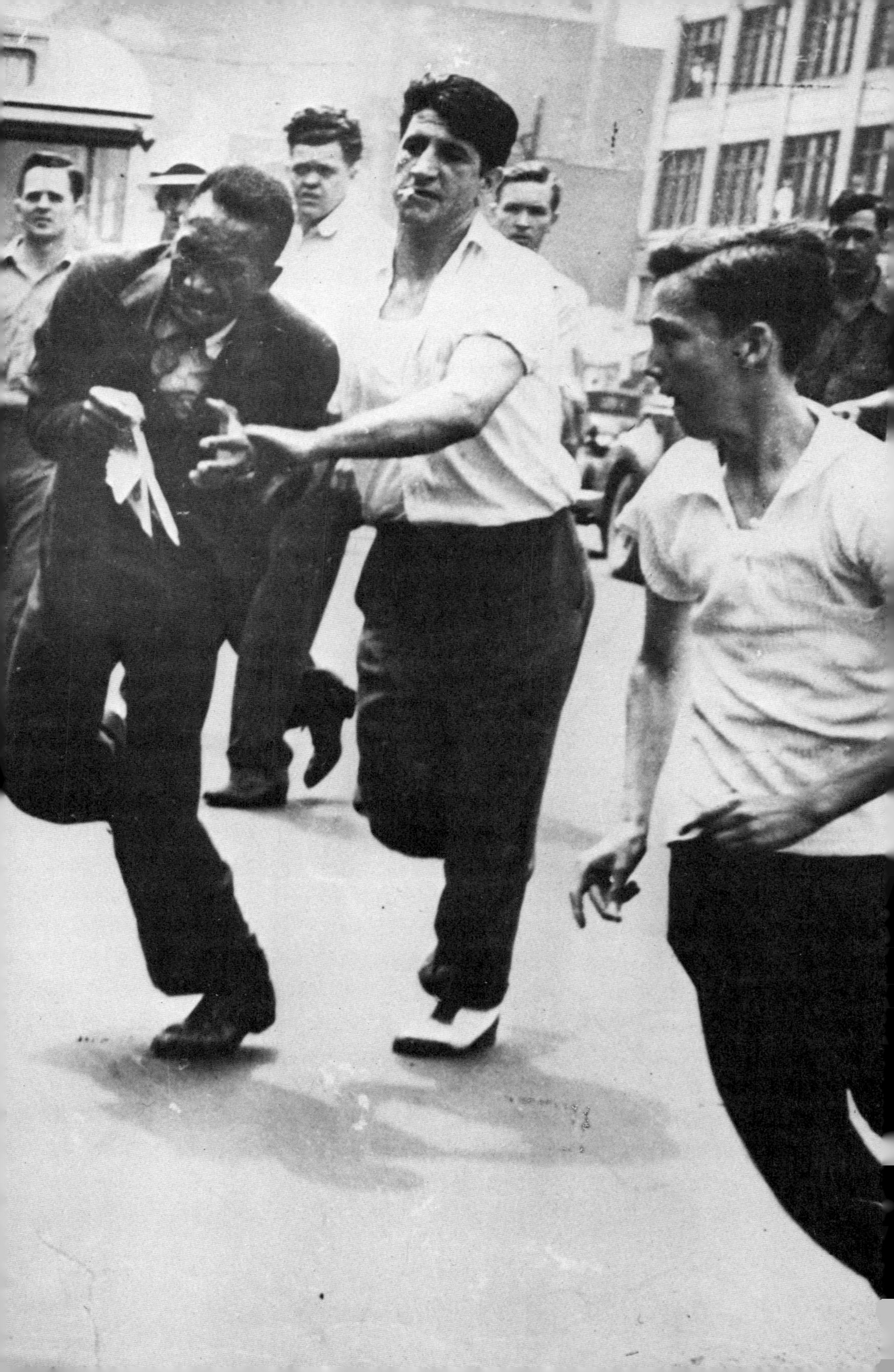

CORE was founded in 1942–43, when certain leaders of the Fellowship of Reconciliation, a pacifist organization, became interested in the use of nonviolent direct action to fight racial discrimination. CORE combined Gandhi's techniques with the sit-in, derived from the sit-down strikes of the 1930s. Until about 1959 CORE's main activity was attacking discrimination in places of public accommodation in the cities of the Northern and Border states. As late as 1961 two-thirds of its membership, and most of its national officers, were white.

Meanwhile, wartime racial disorders had broken out sporadically—in Mobile, Los Angeles, Beaumont, Texas, and elsewhere. The riot in Detroit in 1943 was the most destructive. The Negro population in the city had risen sharply and more than fifty thousand recent arrivals put immense pressures on the housing market. Neighborhood turnover at the edge of the ghetto bred bitterness and sometimes violence, and recreational areas became centers of racial abrasion. The Federal regulations requiring employment standards in defense industries also angered whites; several unauthorized walkouts had occurred in automobile plants after Negro workers were upgraded. The activities in Detroit of several leading spokesmen for white supremacy—Gerald L. K. Smith, Frank J. Norris, and Father Charles Coughlin—inflamed many white Southerners who had migrated to Detroit during the war.

On Sunday, June 20, rioting broke out on Bell Isle, a recreational spot used by both races but predominantly by Negroes. Fist fights escalated into a major conflict. The first wave of looting and bloodshed began in the Negro ghetto, Paradise Valley, and later spread to other sections of the city. Whites began attacking Negroes as they emerged from the city's all-night movie theaters in the downtown area. White

Detroit, 1943

forays into Negro residential areas by car were met by gunfire. By the time Federal troops arrived to halt the racial conflict, twenty-five Negroes and nine whites were dead, property damage exceeded two million dollars, and a legacy of fear and hate had become part of the city.

Again, in 1943, a riot erupted in Harlem, New York, following the attempt of a white policeman to arrest a Negro woman defended by a Negro soldier. Negro rioters assaulted white passersby, overturned parked automobiles, and tossed bricks and bottles at policemen. The major emphasis was on destroying property, looting, and burning stores. Six persons died, over five hundred were injured, and more than a hundred were jailed.

White opinion in some quarters of America had begun to shift to a more sympathetic regard for Negroes during the New Deal, and the war had accelerated that movement. Thoughtful whites had been painfully aware of the contradiction in opposing Nazi racial philosophy with racially segregated military units. In postwar years, American racial attitudes became more liberal as new nonwhite nations emerged in Asia and Africa and took increasing responsibilities in international councils.

In 1947, in conjunction with the Fellowship of Reconciliation, CORE conducted a "Journey of Reconciliation"—which would later be called a Freedom Ride—in the states of the Upper South. The object was to test compliance with the Supreme Court decision outlawing segregation on interstate buses. The resistance met by riders in some areas, and the sentencing of two of them to thirty days on a North Carolina road gang, dramatized the gap between American democratic theory and practice.

The Supreme Court, in *Brown v. Board of Education,* held in 1954 that "separate but equal" schools were inherently unequal and that school districts that had segregated school systems were to abolish segregation with "all deliberate speed." This historic decision became the triumphant climax to the NAACP's campaign against educational segregation in the public schools of the South.

It was on December 1, 1955, that Mrs. Rosa Parks refused to move to the back of a Montgomery, Alabama, bus so that a white man could occupy her seat. Her arrest precipitated a year-long boycott of Montgomery buses. Ninety-eight per cent of the city's Negroes either walked to work or rode in car pools. The boycott captured the imagination of the nation and of the Negro community in particular, and led to the growing use of direct-action techniques. It catapulted into national prominence the Reverend Martin Luther King, Jr., who, like the founders of CORE, held to a Gandhian belief in the principles of pacifism.

The growing size of the Northern Negro vote made civil rights a major issue in national elections and, ultimately, in 1957, led to the establishment of the Federal Civil Rights Commission, which had the power to investigate discriminatory conditions throughout the country and to recommend corrective measures to the President. Northern and Western states outlawed discrimination in employment, housing, and public accommodations. The NAACP, in successive court victories, won judgments against racially restrictive covenants in housing; segregation in interstate transportation; and discrimination in publicly-owned facilities. The NAACP helped register voters.

Even before a court decision obtained by NAACP attorneys in November 1956 desegregated the Montgomery buses, a similar movement had started in Tallahassee, Florida. Afterward another one developed in Birmingham, Alabama. In 1957 the Negroes of Tuskegee, Alabama, undertook a three-

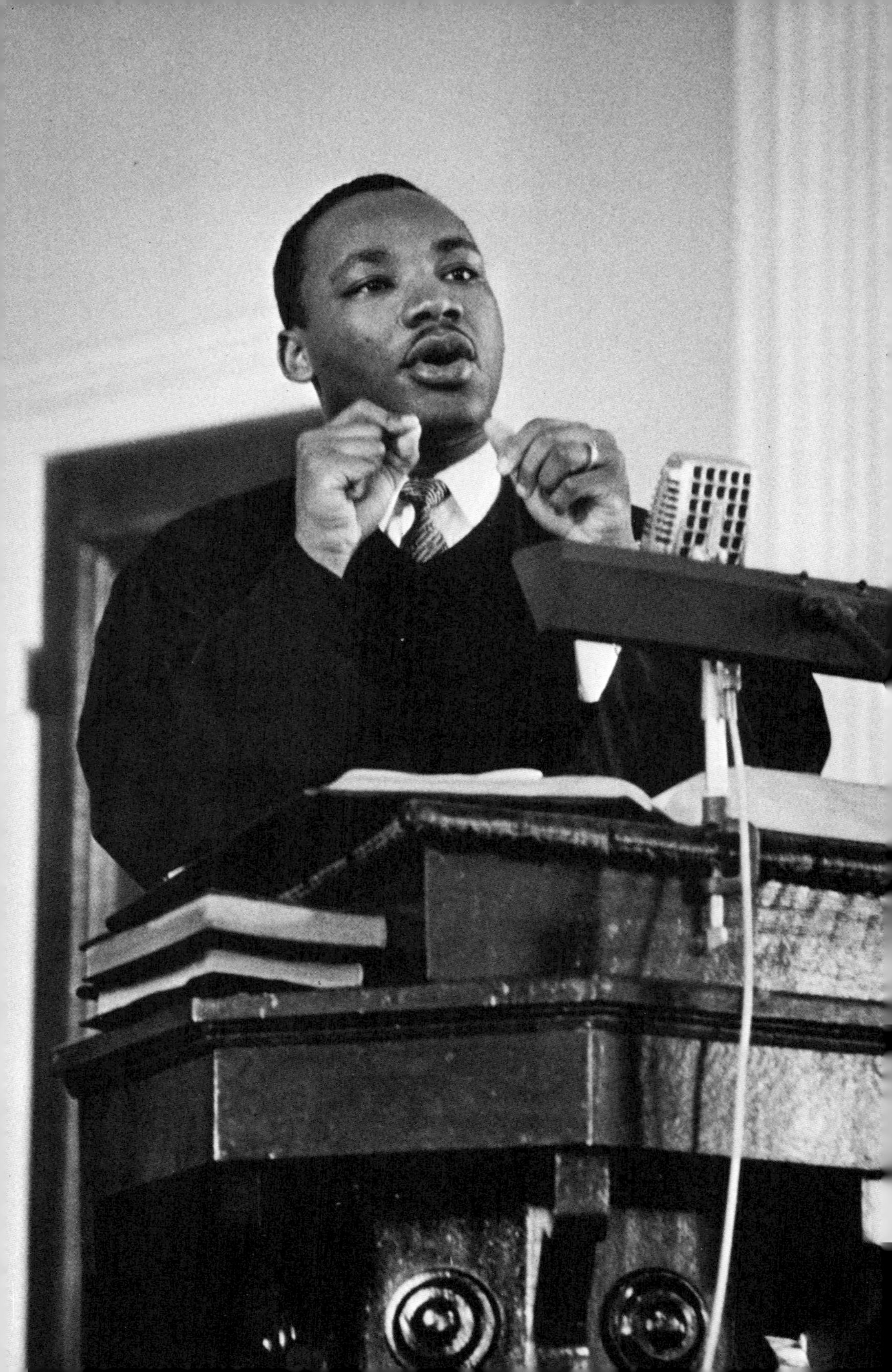

year boycott of local merchants after the state legislature gerrymandered nearly all the Negro voters outside of the town's boundaries. In response to a lawsuit filed by the NAACP, the Supreme Court ruled the Tuskegee gerrymander illegal.

These events were widely heralded. A "new Negro" had emerged in the South—militant, no longer fearful of white hoodlums or mobs, and ready to use his collective weight to achieve his ends.

In this mood, the Reverend Martin Luther King, Jr., established the Southern Christian Leadership Conference in 1957 to coordinate direct-action activities in Southern cities.

Nonviolent direct action attained popularity not only because of the effectiveness of King's leadership but because the older techniques of legal and legislative action had had limited success. Impressive as the advances in the fifteen years after World War II were, and in spite of state laws and Supreme Court decisions, something was still clearly wrong.

Negroes remained disfranchised in most of the South, even though in the twelve years following the outlawing of the white primary in 1944 the number of Negroes registered in Southern states had risen from about 250,000 to nearly 1.25 million.

Supreme Court decisions desegregating transportation facilities were still being largely ignored in the South.

Discrimination in employment and housing continued, not only in the South but also in Northern states having model civil-rights laws.

The Negro unemployment rate moved steadily upward after 1954.

The South reacted to the Supreme Court's decision on school desegregation by attempting to outlaw the NAACP, intimidating civil-rights leaders, calling for "massive resist-

Martin Luther King, Jr.

ance" to the Court's decision, curtailing Negro voter registration, and forming White Citizens' Councils.

At the same time, Negro attitudes were changing. In what has been described as a revolution in expectations, Negroes were gaining a new sense of self-respect and a new self-image as a result of the civil-rights movement and their own advancement. King and others were demonstrating that nonviolent direct action could succeed in the South. New laws and court decisions and the increasing support of white public opinion gave American Negroes a new confidence in the future.

Negroes no longer felt that they had to accept the humiliations of second-class citizenship. Ironically, it was the very successes in the legislatures and the courts that, more perhaps than any other single factor, led to intensified Negro expectations and the resulting dissatisfaction with the limitations of legal and legislative programs. Increasing Negro impatience accounted for the rising tempo of nonviolent direct action in the late 1950s, culminating in the student sit-ins of 1960 and the inauguration of what is popularly known as the Civil Rights Revolution or the Negro Revolt.

Many believe that the Montgomery bus boycott ushered in this Negro Revolt. The importance of the boycott is great, for it focused attention on King and his techniques. But the decisive break with traditional techniques came with the college-student sit-ins that swept the South in the winter and spring of 1960.

In dozens of communities in the Upper South, the Atlantic coastal states, and Texas, student demonstrations secured the desegregation of lunch counters in drug and variety stores. Arrests were numbered in the thousands, and brutality was evident in scores of communities. In the Deep South the campaign ended in failure, even in instances where hun-

Students sitting in at a lunch counter, 1960

dreds had been arrested, as in Montgomery; Orangeburg, South Carolina; and Baton Rouge, Louisiana. But the youth had captured the imagination of the Negro community and to a remarkable extent of the whole nation.

The Negro protest movement would never be the same again. The Southern college students shook the power structure of the Negro community, made direct action temporarily pre-eminent as a civil-rights tactic, speeded up the process of social change in race relations, and ultimately turned the Negro protest organizations toward a deep concern with the economic and social problems of the masses.

A gradual change in tactics to achieve civil-rights goals, and a shift in emphasis on the goals themselves, resulted from the youth involvement in the movement. The shift was from legal to direct action; from middle- and upper-class to mass action; from attempts to guarantee the Negro's Constitutional rights to efforts to secure economic policies giving him equality of opportunity; from appeals to the sense of fair play of white Americans to demands based upon power in the black ghetto.

The successes of the student movement threatened existing Negro leadership and precipitated a spirited rivalry among civil-rights organizations. The NAACP and SCLC (Southern Christian Leadership Conference) associated themselves with the student movement. The organizing meeting of the Student Nonviolent Coordinating Committee (SNCC) at Raleigh, North Carolina, in April 1960 was called by Martin Luther King, but within a year the youth considered King too cautious and broke with him.

The NAACP now decided to make direct action a major part of its strategy, and organized and reactivated college and youth chapters in the Southern and Border states.

CORE, still unknown to the general public, installed James

Farmer as national director in January 1961, and that spring joined the front rank of civil-rights organizations with the famous Freedom Ride to Alabama and Mississippi. Negroes and whites rode side by side on an interstate bus ride and defied segregation practices in bus-station waiting rooms and restaurants. The Freedom Ride dramatized the persistence of segregated public transportation. A bus was burned in Alabama, and hundreds of demonstrators spent a month or more in Mississippi prisons. Finally, a new order from the Interstate Commerce Commission desegregating all interstate transportation facilities received partial compliance.

Disagreement over strategy and tactics inevitably became intertwined with personal and organizational rivalries. Each civil-rights group felt the need for proper credit in order to obtain the prestige and financial contributions necessary to maintain and expand its own programs. The local and national, individual and organizational clashes only stimulated competition and activity, which further accelerated the pace of social change. Yet there were differences in style.

CORE was the most interracial of the groups. SCLC appeared to be the most deliberate. SNCC staff workers lived on subsistence allowances and seemed to regard going to jail as a way of life.

The NAACP continued the most varied programs, retaining a strong emphasis on court litigation, maintaining a highly effective lobby at the national capital, and engaging in direct-action campaigns.

The National Urban League, under the leadership of Whitney M. Young, Jr., appointed executive director in 1961, became more outspoken and talked more firmly to businessmen who had previously been treated with utmost tact and caution.

The role of whites in the protest movement gradually

Malcolm X instructing a class of Black Muslims

changed. Instead of occupying positions of leadership, they found themselves relegated to the role of followers. Whites were likely to be suspect in the activist organizations. Negroes had come to feel less dependent on whites, more confident of their own power, and they demanded that their leaders be black.

The NAACP had long since acquired Negro leadership but continued to welcome white liberal support. SCLC and SNCC were from the start Negro-led and Negro-dominated. CORE became predominantly Negro as it expanded in 1962 and 1963; today all executives are Negro, and a constitutional amendment adopted in 1965 officially limited white leadership in the chapters.

A major factor intensifying the civil-rights movement was widespread Negro unemployment and poverty. An important force in awakening Negro protest was the meteoric rise to national prominence of the Black Muslims, believers in the religion of the Arabian prophet Mohammed. The organization, established around 1930, reached the peak of its influence when more progress toward equal rights was being made than ever before in American history, and yet, at the same time, economic opportunity for the poorest groups in the urban ghettos was stagnating.

The Black Muslims preached a vision of the doom of the white "devils" and the coming dominance of the black man. They promised a utopian paradise of a separate territory within the United States for a Negro state, and offered a practical program of building Negro business through hard work, thrift, and racial unity.

To those willing to submit to the rigid discipline of the movement, the Black Muslims organization gave a sense of purpose and dignity.

In 1963, as the direct-action tactics took more dramatic form and the civil-rights groups began to articulate the needs of the masses and draw some of them to their demonstrations, the protest movement assumed a new note of urgency, a demand for complete "Freedom Now!"

Direct action returned to the Northern cities, taking the form of massive protests against economic, housing, and educational inequities, and a fresh wave of demonstrations swept the South from Cambridge, Maryland, to Birmingham, Alabama. Northern Negroes launched street demonstrations against discrimination in the building trade unions and, the following winter, school boycotts against *de facto* segregation.

In the North 1963 and 1964 brought the beginning of the waves of civil disorders in Northern urban centers. In the South there were incidents of brutal white resistance to the civil-rights movement, beginning with the murder of Mississippi Negro leader Medgar Evers, and of four Negro schoolgirls, victims of the Sunday-morning bombing of a church in Birmingham.

The massive anti-Negro resistance in Birmingham and numerous other Southern cities during the spring of 1963 compelled the nation to face the problem of race prejudice in the South. President Kennedy affirmed that racial discrimination was a moral issue and asked Congress for a major civil-rights bill.

But the chief impetus for what was to be the Civil Rights Act of 1964 was the March on Washington in August 1963.

Early in the year, A. Philip Randolph issued a call for a March on Washington to dramatize the need for jobs and to press for a Federal commitment to job action. At about the same time, Protestant, Jewish, and Catholic churches sought and obtained representation on the March committee. Although the AFL-CIO national council refused to endorse the March, a number of labor leaders and international unions participated.

Reversing an earlier stand, President Kennedy approved the March. A quarter of a million people, about 20 per cent of them white, participated. It was more than a summation of the past years of struggle and aspiration. It symbolized certain new directions: a deeper concern for the economic problems of the masses; more involvement of white moderates; and new demands from the most militant, who implied that only a revolutionary change in American institutions would permit Negroes to achieve the dignity of citizens.

President Kennedy had set the stage for the Civil Rights Act of 1964. After his death, President Johnson took forceful and effective action to secure its enactment.

The law settled the public-accommodations issue in the South's major cities. Its voting section, however, promised more than it could accomplish. Martin Luther King, Jr., and SCLC dramatized the issue locally with demonstrations at Selma, Alabama, in the spring of 1965. Again the national government was forced to intervene, and a new and more effective voting law was passed.

Birmingham had made direct action respectable; Selma, which drew thousands of white moderates from the North, made direct action fashionable. Yet as early as 1964 it was becoming evident that, like legal action, direct action was an instrument of limited usefulness.

In Deep South states such as Mississippi and Alabama direct action had failed to desegregate public accommodations in the sit-ins of 1960–61. A major reason was that Negroes lacked the leverage of the vote. The demonstrations of the early 1960s had been successful principally in places

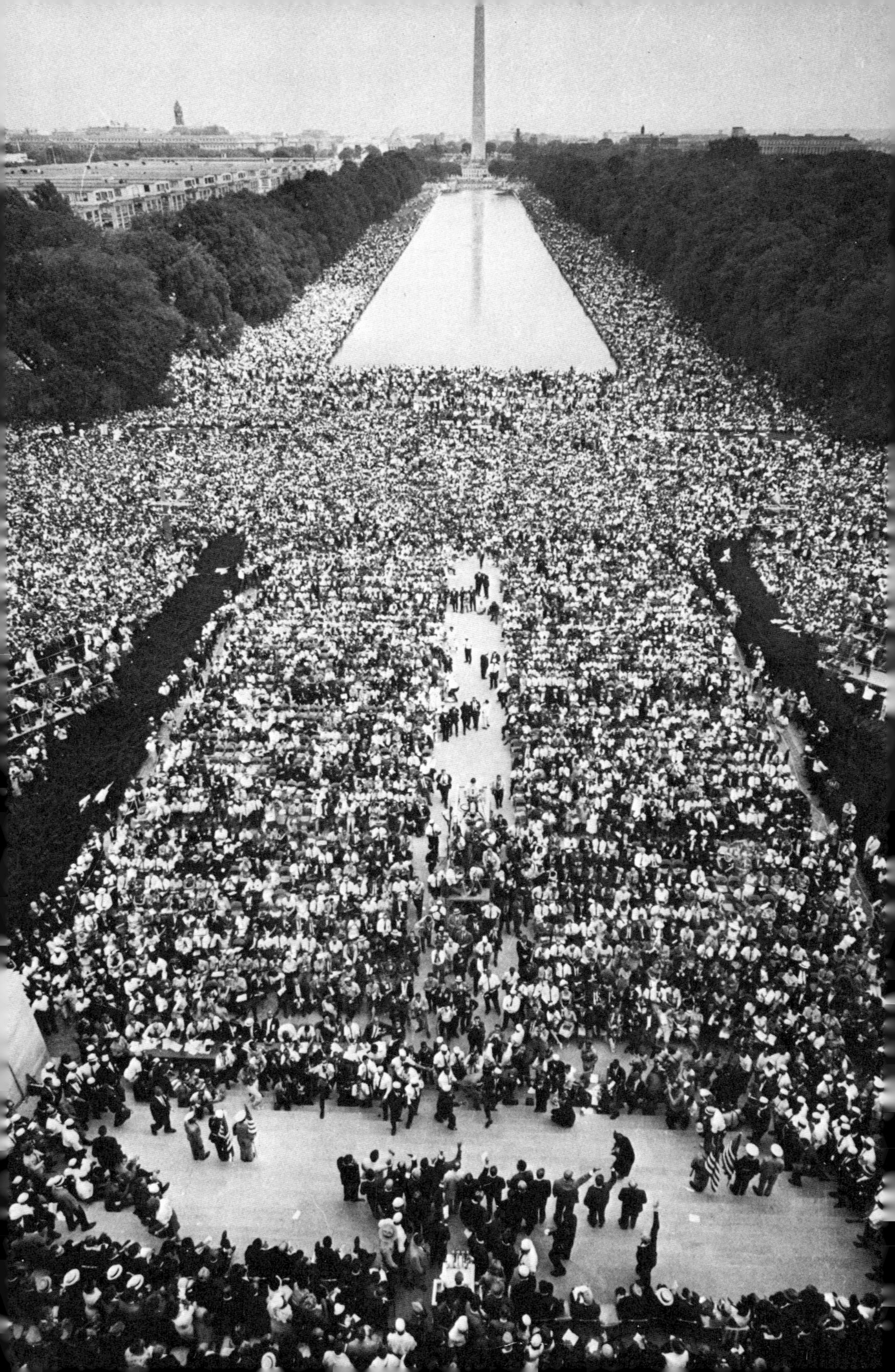

such as Atlanta; Nashville, Tennessee; Durham and Winston-Salem, North Carolina; Louisville, Kentucky; Savannah; New Orleans; Charleston; and Dallas—where Negroes voted and could swing elections.

Beginning in 1961, Robert Moses of SNCC, with the cooperation of CORE and the NAACP, established voter-registration projects in the cities and county seats of Mississippi. He succeeded in registering only a handful of Negroes, but by 1964 he had generated enough support throughout the country to enable the Mississippi Freedom Democratic Party, which he had created, to challenge dramatically the seating of the official white delegates from the state at the Democratic National Convention.

In the black ghettos of the North direct action also largely failed. Street demonstrations did compel employers, from supermarkets to banks, to add many Negroes to their work force in Northern and Western cities, in some Southern cities, and even in some Southern towns where Negroes had considerable buying power. However, separate and inferior schools, slum housing, and police hostility proved invulnerable to direct attack.

Although Negroes were being hired in increasing numbers, mass unemployment and underemployment remained. As economist Vivian Henderson pointed out in his testimony before the Commission:

> No one can deny that all Negroes have benefited from civil-rights laws and desegregation in public life in one way or another. The fact is, however, that the masses of Negroes have not experienced tangible benefits in a significant way. This is so in education and housing. It is critically so in the area of jobs and economic security. Expectations of Negro masses for equal-job-opportunity programs have fallen far short of fulfillment. Negroes have made gains. . . . There have been important gains. But . . . the masses of Negroes have been virtually untouched by those gains.

March on Washington, 1963

Faced with the intransigence of the Deep South and the inadequacy of direct action to solve the problems of the slum dwellers, Negro protest organizations began to diverge. The momentum toward unity apparent in 1963 was lost. At the very time that white support for the protest movement was rising markedly, militant Negroes felt increasingly isolated from the American scene. On two things, however, all segments of the protest movement agreed:

Future civil-rights activity would have to focus on the economic and social discrimination in the urban ghettos.

While demonstrations would still have a place, the major weapon would have to be the political potential of the black masses.

By the middle of the decade many militant Negro members of SNCC and CORE had begun to turn away from American society and the "middle-class way of life." Cynical about the liberals and the leaders of organized labor, they regarded compromise, even as a temporary tactical device, as anathema. They talked more of "revolutionary" changes in the social structure, of retaliatory violence, and increasingly rejected white assistance. They insisted that Negro power alone could compel the white "ruling class" to make concessions.

Yet they also spoke of an alliance of Negroes and unorganized lower-class whites to overthrow the "power structure" of capitalists, politicians, and bureaucratic labor leaders who exploited the poor of both races by dividing them through an appeal to race prejudice.

At the same time that activities of Negro militants declined, other issues, particularly Vietnam, diverted the attention of the country, and of some Negro leaders, from the issue of equality. Reduced financing made it increasingly difficult for civil-rights organizations to support staff personnel. Most important was the increasing frustration of expectations that affected the direct-action advocates of the early 1960s—the sense of futility growing out of the feeling that progress had turned out to be tokenism, that the compromises of the white community were sedatives rather than solutions, and that the current methods of Negro protest were doing little for the masses of the race.

As frustrations grew, the ideology and rhetoric of a number of civil-rights activists became angrier. One man more than any other—a black man who grew up believing whites had murdered his father—became the spokesman for this anger: Malcolm X of the Black Muslims. He perhaps best embodied the belief that racism was so deeply ingrained in white America that appeals to conscience would bring no fundamental change.

In this setting, the rhetoric of Black Power developed.

The precipitating occasion was the march of James Meredith from Memphis, Tennessee, to Jackson, Mississippi, in June 1966. Meredith hoped to demonstrate that a Negro could walk in the South without fear. But he was shot and wounded by a white man and civil-rights workers from all over the country rushed to Mississippi to take up his walk.

Black Power first articulated a mood rather than a program. The mood was one of disillusionment and alienation from white America, and also one of independence, race pride, and self-respect—or "black consciousness." Having become a household phrase, the term generated intense discussion of its real meaning, and a broad spectrum of ideologies and programmatic proposals emerged.

In politics Black Power meant independent action—Negro control of the political power of the black ghettos, and its use to improve economic and social conditions. It could take the form of organizing a black political party or controlling the political machinery within the ghetto without the guidance or support of white politicians. Where predominantly Negro areas lacked Negroes in elective office, whether in the rural Black Belt of the South or in the urban centers, Black Power advocates sought the election of Negroes through voter-registration campaigns, by getting out the vote, and by working for the redrawing of electoral districts. The basic belief was that only a well-organized and cohesive bloc of Negro voters could provide for the needs of the black masses. Even some Negro politicians allied to the major political parties adopted the term "Black Power" to describe their interest in the Negro vote.

In economic terms Black Power meant creating independent, self-sufficient Negro business enterprise, not only by encouraging Negro entrepreneurs but also by forming Negro cooperatives in the ghettos and in the predominantly black rural counties of the South. In the area of education Black Power called for local community control of the public schools in the black ghettos.

Throughout, the emphasis was on self-help, racial unity, and among the most militant, retaliatory violence. The latter ranged from the legal right of self-defense to attempts to justify looting and arson in ghetto riots, guerrilla warfare, and armed rebellion.

Phrases such as "Black Power," "black consciousness," and "Black is beautiful" enjoyed an extensive currency in the Negro community, even within the NAACP and among relatively conservative politicians—but particularly among young intellectuals and Afro-American student groups on predominantly white college campuses. Expressed in its most extreme form by small, often local, fringe groups, the Black Power ideology became associated with SNCC and CORE.

Negroes strive for Black Power in politics (top) and in public education.

Generally regarded as the most militant among the important Negro protest organizations, SNCC and CORE have different interpretations of the Black Power doctrine.

SNCC calls for totally independent political action outside the established political parties, as with the Black Panther Party in Lowndes County, Alabama. SNCC rejects political alliances with other groups until Negroes have themselves built a substantial base of independent political power, applauds the idea of guerrilla warfare, and regards riots as rebellions.

CORE has been more flexible. Approving the SNCC strategy, it also advocates working within the Democratic Party and forming alliances with other groups. And while seeking to justify riots as the natural explosion of an oppressed people against intolerable conditions, CORE advocates violence only in self-defense. Both groups favor cooperatives, but CORE has seemed more inclined toward job-training programs and developing a Negro entrepreneurial class based upon the market within the black ghettos.

What is new about Black Power is phraseology rather than substance.

Black consciousness has roots in the organization of Negro churches and mutual benefit societies in the early days of the republic. The latter first appeared when Northern free Negroes formed associations to provide assistance to members in time of economic distress, illness, and death. Black consciousness also underlaid the antebellum Negro Convention Movement; the Negro colonization schemes of the nineteenth century; Du Bois's concept of Pan-Africanism with its feeling of close kinship of black Americans with Asian and African peoples trying to break out of European colonial systems; Booker T. Washington's advocacy of race pride, self-help, and racial solidarity; the Harlem Renaissance; and the Garvey movement. The decade after World War I—which saw the militant, race-proud "new Negro," the relatively widespread theory of retaliatory violence, and the high tide of the Negro-support-of-Negro-business ideology—exhibits striking parallels with the 1960s.

The theme of retaliatory violence is hardly new to American Negroes. Most racial disorders in American history, until recent years, were characterized by white attacks on Negroes. But Negroes have retaliated violently in the past.

Black Power rhetoric and ideology actually express a lack of power. The slogan emerged when the Negro protest movement was slowing down, when it was finding increasing resistance to its changing goals, when it discovered that nonviolent direct action was no more a panacea than legal action, when CORE and SNCC were declining in terms of activity, membership, and financial support.

This combination of circumstances provoked anger deepened by impotence. Powerless to make any fundamental changes—powerless, that is, to compel white America to make those changes—many advocates of Black Power have retreated into an unreal world, where they see an outnumbered and poverty-stricken minority organizing itself independently of whites and creating sufficient power to force white America to grant its demands. To date, the evidence suggests that the situation is much like that of the 1840s, when a small group of intellectuals advocated slave insurrections but stopped short of organizing them.

The Black Power advocates of today consciously feel that they are the most militant group in the Negro protest movement. Yet they have retreated from a direct confrontation with American society on the issue of integration and, by preaching separatism, unconsciously function as an accommodation of white racism. Much of their economic program, as well as their interest in Negro history, self-help, racial solidarity, and separation is reminiscent of Booker T. Washington. The rhetoric is different, but the programs are remarkably similar.

By 1967 whites could point to the demise of slavery, the decline of illiteracy among Negroes, the legal protection provided by the Constitutional amendments and civil-rights legislation, and the growing size of the Negro middle class. Whites would call it Negro progress from slavery to freedom toward equality.

Negroes could point to the doctrine of white supremacy, its widespread acceptance, its persistence after emancipation, and its influence on the definition of the place of Negroes in American life. They could point to their long fight for full citizenship, when they had active opposition from most of the white population and little or no support from the government. They could see progress toward equality accompanied by bitter resistance.

Perhaps most of all, they could feel the persistent, pervasive racism that kept them in inferior segregated schools, restricted them to ghettos, barred them from fair employment, provided double standards in courts of justice, inflicted bodily harm on their children, and blighted their lives with a sense of hopelessness and despair.

In all of this and in the context of professed ideals, Negroes would find more retrogression than progress, more rejection than acceptance.

Until the middle of the twentieth century the course of Negro protest movements in the United States, except for slave revolts, was based in the cities of the North, where Negroes enjoyed sufficient freedom to mount a sustained protest. It was in the cities, North and South, that Negroes had their greatest independence and mobility. It was natural, therefore, for black protest movements to be urban-based—and, until the last dozen years or so, limited to the North.

As Negroes migrated from the South, the mounting strength of their votes in Northern cities became a vital element in drawing the Federal government into the defense of the civil rights of Southern Negroes. While rural Negroes today face great racial problems, the major unsolved questions that touch the core of Negro life stem from discrimination embedded in urban housing, employment, and education.

Over the years the character of Negro protest has changed. Originally it was a white liberal and Negro upper-class movement aimed at securing the Constitutional rights of Negroes through propaganda, lawsuits, and legislation. In recent years the emphasis in tactics shifted first to direct action and then—among the most militant—to the rhetoric of Black Power. The role of white liberals declined as Negroes came to direct the struggle. At the same time, the Negro protest movement became more of a mass movement, with increasing participation from the working classes.

As these changes were occurring, and while substantial progress was being made to secure Constitutional rights for Negroes, the goals of the movement were broadened. Protest groups now demand special efforts to overcome the Negro's poverty and cultural deprivation—conditions that cannot be erased simply by ensuring Constitutional rights.

The central thrust of Negro protest in the current period has aimed at the inclusion of Negroes in American society on the basis of full equality rather than at a fundamental transformation of American institutions. There have been elements calling for a revolutionary overthrow of the American social system or for a complete withdrawal of Negroes

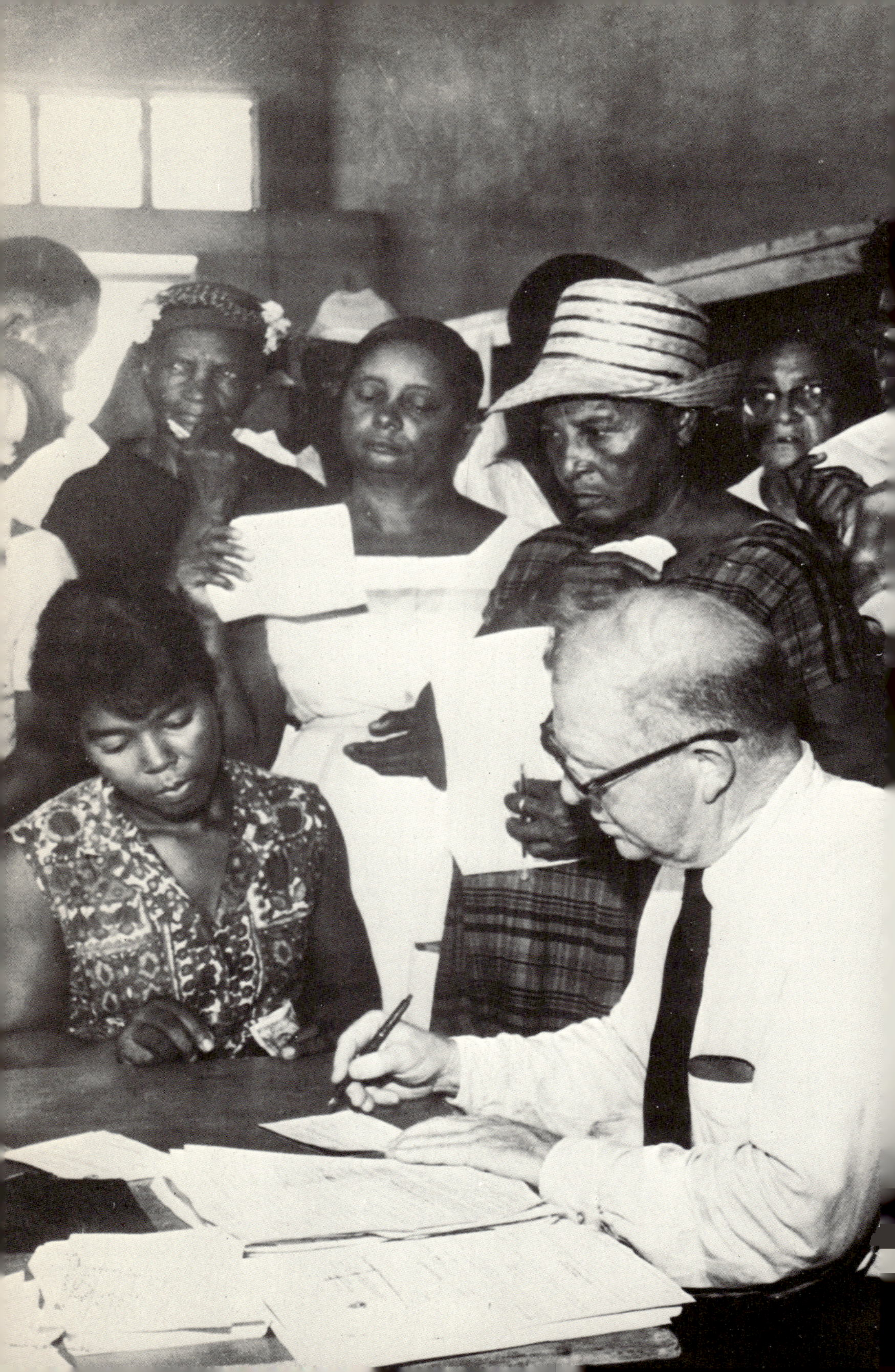

from American society. But these solutions have had little popular support.

Negro protest, for the most part, has been firmly rooted in the basic values of American society, seeking not their destruction but their fulfillment.

Negroes registering to vote in Mississippi, 1966

How to Build a Ghetto

Throughout this century, but particularly in the last thirty years, the Negro population of the United States has been steadily moving from rural areas to urban areas, and from the South to the North and the West.

In 1910 almost 3 million Negroes (less than one third of the total Negro population at the time) lived in American cities. Today, about 15 million Negro Americans (almost 70 per cent of the present Negro population of over 21 million) live in metropolitan areas.

In 1910 only about 9 per cent of the Negro population lived outside the South. Today, almost 10 million, or close to one half of the country's Negro citizens, live in the North or the West.

Three basic trends have caused these shifts in population:

A rapid increase in the size of the Negro population.
A continuous flow of Negroes from Southern rural areas, partly

to large cities in the South, but primarily to large cities in the North and West.

An increasing concentration of Negroes in large metropolitan areas within racially segregated neighborhoods.

Taken together, these trends have produced large and constantly growing concentrations of black Americans within cities in all parts of the nation. Because most major civil disorders of recent years have occurred in predominantly Negro neighborhoods, we have examined the causes of this concentration.

During the first half of this century the white population of the United States grew at a slightly faster rate than did the Negro population. The proportion of Negroes in the country declined from 12 per cent in 1900 to 10 per cent in 1940.

This was so because the live-birth rate among Negroes was offset by the death rate among Negroes; and because the white population was increased by large-scale immigration of whites from Europe.

But by the end of World War II the Negro death rate had decreased, and it has continued to drop at an increasing rate since then. Major advances in medicine and medical care together with the increasing youth of the Negro population have been responsible for this. In addition, white immigration from outside the United States dropped dramatically after stringent restrictions were adopted in the 1920s. Thus, by mid-century, both factors (the high death rate among Negroes and the large numbers of white immigrants) which had previously offset higher birth rates among Negro women were no longer in effect.

While Negro birth rates have declined sharply in the past ten years, white birth rates have declined even more. Negro rates are much higher in comparison. The result is that the Negro population is now growing significantly faster than the white population.

In 1950 at least one of every ten Americans was Negro; in 1966 one in nine. (This estimation is undoubtedly too low because the Census Bureau has consistently undercounted the number of Negroes in the United States by as much as 10 per cent.) If this trend continues, one of every eight Americans will be Negro by 1972.

Another consequence of higher birth rates among Negroes is that the Negro population is considerably younger than the white population. In 1966 slightly more than one third of the white population was under eighteen years of age, as compared to nearly one half of the Negro population. About one of every six children under five years of age and one of every six new babies are Negro.

Negro-white birth rates bear an interesting relationship to

educational experience. Negro women having low levels of education have more children than white women who have had similar schooling, while Negro women with four years or more of college education have fewer children than white women similarly educated.

This suggests that the difference between Negro and white birth rates may decline in the future if Negro educational attainment compares more closely with that of whites, and if a rising proportion of members of both groups complete college.

Negro migration from the South began after the Civil War. By the turn of the century, sizable Negro populations lived in many large Northern cities. Philadelphia, for example, had 63,400 Negro residents in 1900.

The movement of Negroes out of the rural South accelerated during World War I, when floods and boll weevils hurt farming in the South, and the industrial demands of the war created thousands of new jobs for unskilled workers in the North. After the war the shift to mechanized farming spurred the continuing movement of Negroes from rural Southern areas.

The Depression slowed this migratory flow, but World War II set it in motion again.

More recently, continuing mechanization of agriculture and the expansion of industrial employment in Northern and Western cities have served to sustain the movement of Negroes out of the South—although at a slightly lower rate.

The highest rate of Negro migration was reached during the World War II decade, when slightly more than 1.5 million Negroes left the South. This scale of migration is relatively small when compared to the earlier waves of European immigrants. Between 1901 and 1911, 8.8 million immigrants

Negro migration: from the front porches of the South to the sidewalks of the North

entered the United States; another 5.7 million arrived during the following decade. Even during the years from 1960 through 1966 there were three times as many immigrants from abroad as Negro migrants within the United States.

Three major routes of Negro migration from the South have developed. One runs north along the Atlantic seaboard toward Boston, another north from Mississippi toward Chicago, and the third west from Texas and Louisiana toward California.

The flow of Negroes from the South has caused the Negro population to grow more rapidly in the North and West. As a result, although a much higher proportion of Negroes still reside in the South, the distribution of Negroes throughout the United States is beginning to approximate that of whites.

Negroes in the North and West are now so numerous that natural increase, rather than migration, provides the greater part of Negro population gains there. And even though Negro migration has continued at a high level, it is responsible for a constantly declining proportion of Negro growth in these regions. In other words, we have reached the point where the Negro populations of the North and West will continue to expand significantly even if migration from the South drops substantially.

Despite accelerating Negro migration from the South, the Negro population there has continued to rise. Nor is it likely to halt. Negro birth rates in the South, as elsewhere, have fallen sharply since 1957. But even if Negro birth rates continue to fall, they are likely to remain high enough to support significant migration to other regions for some time to come. In short, Negro migration from the South, which has maintained a high rate for the past sixty years, will continue unless economic conditions change dramatically in either the South or the North and West.

Statistically, the Negro population in America has become more urbanized, and more metropolitan, than the white population. According to Census Bureau estimates, almost 70 per cent of all Negroes in 1966 lived in metropolitan areas, as compared to 64 per cent of all whites. In the South, more than half the Negro population now lives in cities.

Basic data concerning Negro urbanization trends indicate that:

Almost all Negro population growth is occurring within metropolitan areas, and primarily within central cities. (A central city is that part of a large metropolitan area that contains a recognized large population nucleus of at least fifty thousand inhabitants.)

The vast majority of white population growth is occurring in suburban portions of metropolitan areas. Between 1950 and 1966 central cities received less than 3 per cent of the total white population increase.

As a result, central cities are steadily becoming more heavily Negro, while the urban fringes around them remain almost entirely white.

The Negro population is growing faster, both absolutely and relatively, in the larger metropolitan areas than in the smaller ones.

The twelve largest central cities now contain over two thirds of the Negro population outside the South, and almost one third of the total Negro population in the United States. In early 1968 seven of these cities were almost one-third Negro. Washington, D.C., was two-thirds Negro.

The early pattern of Negro settlement within each metropolitan area followed that of immigrant groups. Migrants converged on the older sections of the central city because the lowest-cost housing was located there, friends and relatives were likely to be living there, and the older neighborhoods at that time often had good public transportation.

But the later phases of Negro settlement and expansion in metropolitan areas diverge sharply from those typical of white immigrants.

As whites were absorbed by the larger society many left their predominantly ethnic neighborhoods and moved to outlying areas to obtain newer housing and better schools. Some scattered randomly over the suburban area. Others established new ethnic clusters in the suburbs, but even these rarely contained solely members of a single ethnic group. As a result, most middle-class neighborhoods—both in the suburbs and within central cities—have no distinctive ethnic character, except that they are white.

Nowhere has the expansion of America's urban Negro population followed this pattern of dispersal. Thousands of Negro families have attained incomes, living standards, and cultural levels matching or surpassing those of whites who have "upgraded" themselves from distinctly ethnic neighborhoods. Yet most Negro families have remained within predominantly Negro neighborhoods, primarily because they have been effectively excluded from white residential areas.

Their exclusion has been accomplished through various discriminatory practices, some obvious and overt, others subtle and hidden. Deliberate efforts are sometimes made to discourage Negro families from purchasing or renting homes in all-white neighborhoods. Intimidation and threats of violence have ranged from throwing garbage on lawns and making threatening phone calls to burning crosses in yards and even dynamiting property. More often, real-estate agents simply refuse to show homes to Negro buyers.

Many middle-class Negro families, therefore, cease looking for homes beyond all-Negro areas or nearby "changing" neighborhoods. For them, trying to move into all-white neighborhoods is not worth the psychological efforts and costs required.

Another form of discrimination, just as significant, is the white withdrawal from, or refusal to enter, neighborhoods to which large numbers of Negroes are moving or have already moved. With normal population turnover, about 20 per cent of the residents of average United States neighborhoods move out every year because of income changes, job transfers, changes in family size and needs, or deaths. The normal turnover rate is even higher in apartment areas. The refusal of whites to move into changing areas when vacancies occur there from normal turnover means that most of these vacancies are eventually occupied by Negroes. An inexorable shift toward heavy Negro occupancy results.

Once this happens, the remaining whites seek to leave, thus confirming the existing belief among whites that complete transformation of a neighborhood is inevitable once Negroes begin to enter. Since the belief itself is one of the major causes of the transformation, it becomes a self-fulfilling prophecy which inhibits the development of racially integrated neighborhoods.

As a result, Negro settlements expand almost entirely through "massive racial transition" at the edges of existing all-Negro neighborhoods, rather than by a gradual dispersion of population throughout the metropolitan area.

Does massive transition occur because of the panic or flight of the original white residents of a neighborhood into which Negroes begin to move? Not necessarily. All that is required for the transition is the failure or refusal of other whites to fill the vacancies resulting from normal turnover. Thus, efforts to stop massive transition by persuading present white residents to remain will ultimately fail unless

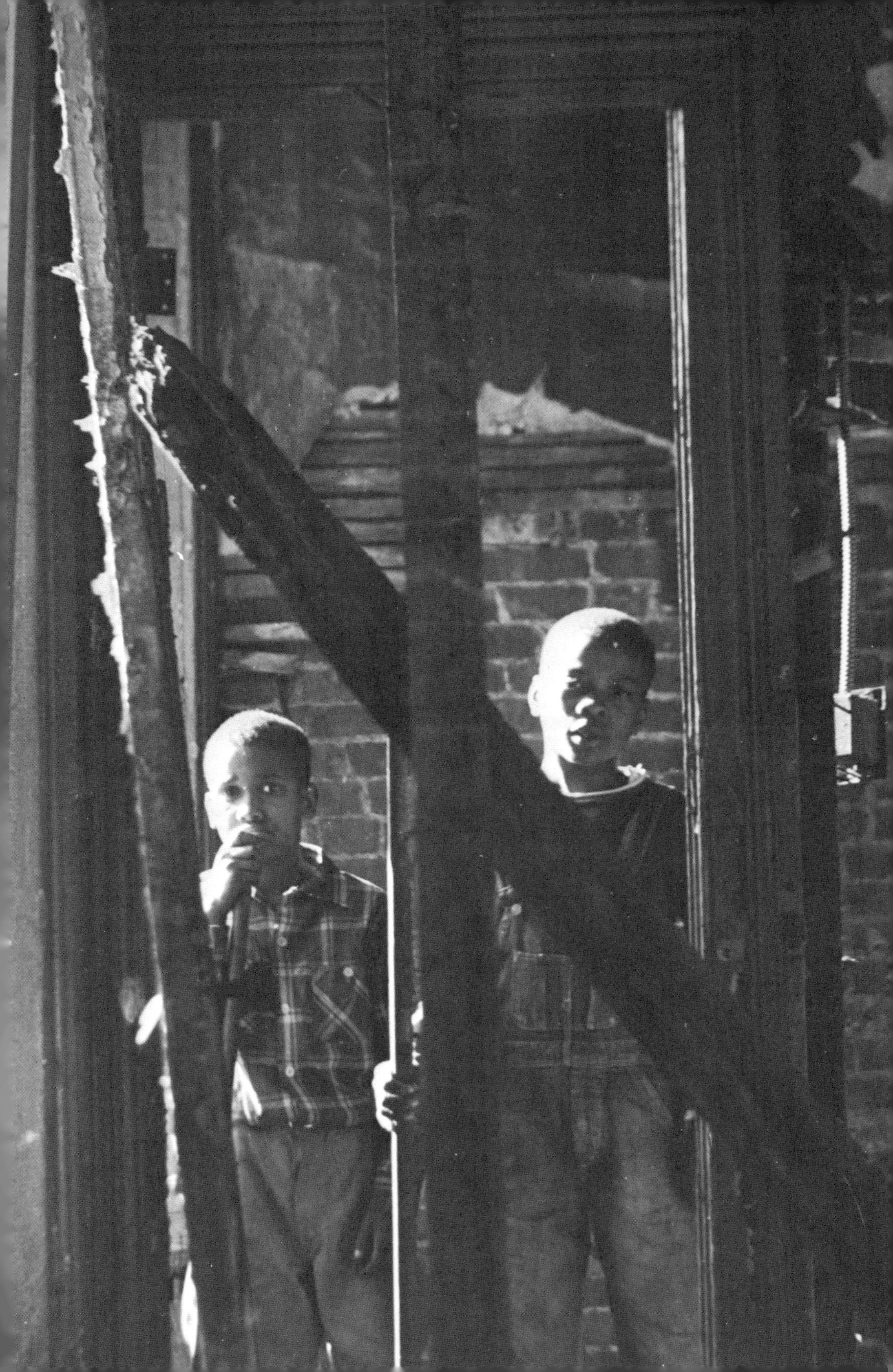

whites outside the neighborhood can be persuaded to move in.

It is obviously true that some residential separation of whites and Negroes would occur even without discriminatory practices by whites. This would result from the desires of some Negroes to live in predominantly Negro neighborhoods, and from differences in meaningful social variables, such as income and educational levels. But these factors alone would not lead to the almost complete segregation of whites and Negroes which has developed in our metropolitan areas.

The process of racial transition in central-city neighborhoods has been only one factor among many others causing millions of whites to move out of central cities as the Negro populations there expanded. More basic, perhaps, have been the rising mobility and affluence of white middle-class families and the more attractive living conditions—particularly the better schools—available to them in the suburbs.

The rapid expansion of all-Negro residential areas and large-scale white withdrawal from them have continued a pattern of residential segregation that has existed in American cities for decades. A study, *Negroes in Cities,* by Karl and Alma Taeuber (published in 1965), reveals that the segregation pattern is present to a high degree in every large city.

A recent Census Bureau study shows that in most of the twelve large cities where special censuses were taken in the mid-1960s, the proportions of Negroes living in neighborhoods of greatest Negro concentration had increased since 1960.

Residential segregation is generally more prevalent with respect to Negroes than to any other minority group, including Puerto Ricans, Orientals, and Mexican-Americans. Moreover, it varies little between central city and suburb.

This nearly universal pattern cannot be explained in terms

of economic discrimination against all low-income groups. Analysis of fifteen representative cities indicates that white upper- and middle-income households are far more segregated from Negro upper- and middle-income households than from white lower-income households.

In summary, the concentration of Negroes in central cities results from a combination of forces. Some of these forces, such as migration and initial settlement patterns in older neighborhoods, are similar to those which affected previous ethnic minorities. Others—particularly discrimination in employment and segregation in housing and schools—are a result of white attitudes based on race and color. These forces continue to shape the future of the central city.

The Disorganized Society

The Negro population in our country is as diverse in income, occupation, family composition, and other variables as the white community. Nevertheless, for purposes of analysis, three major Negro economic groups can be identified.

The first and smallest group consists of middle- and upper-income individuals and households whose educational, occupational, and cultural characteristics are similar to those of middle- and upper-income white groups.

The second and largest group contains Negroes whose incomes are above the "poverty level" but who have not attained the educational, occupational, or income status typical of middle-class Americans.

The third group has very low educational, occupational, and income attainments and lives below the "poverty level."

A recent compilation of data on American Negroes by the Department of Labor and Commerce shows that although incomes of both Negroes and whites have been rising rapidly,

Negro incomes still remain far below those of whites.

Negro family income is not keeping pace with white family income growth.

The Negro upper-income group is expanding rapidly and achieving sizable income gains. From 1960 to 1966 the proportion of Negroes employed in high-skill, high-status, and well-paying jobs rose faster than did comparable proportions among whites.

As Negro incomes have risen, the size of the lowest-income group has grown smaller, and the middle- and upper-income groups have grown larger—both relatively and absolutely.

About two thirds of the lowest-income group—this comprises 20 per cent of all Negro families, though only slightly over 1 per cent of the nation's total population—are making no significant economic gains despite continued general prosperity. Half of these hard-core disadvantaged—more than two million persons

—live in central-city neighborhoods. Here unemployment rates have declined only slightly. The proportion of families with female heads has increased. Housing conditions have worsened even though rents have gone up.

The capacity to obtain and hold a "good job" is the traditional test of participation in American society. Steady employment with adequate compensation provides both purchasing power and social status. It develops the capabilities, confidence, and self-esteem an individual needs to be a responsible citizen, and it provides a basis for a stable family life.

To quote Daniel P. Moynihan, prominent educator and director of the Joint Center of Urban Studies (Massachusetts Institute of Technology and Harvard University):

> The principal measure of progress toward equality will be that of employment. It is the primary source of individual or group identity. In America what you do is what you are: To do nothing is to be nothing; to do little is to be little. The equations are implacable and blunt, and ruthlessly public.
>
> For the Negro American it is already, and will continue to be, the master problem. It is the measure of white *bona fides*. It is the measure of Negro competence, and also of the competence of American society. Most importantly, the linkage between problems of employment and the range of social pathology that afflicts the Negro community is unmistakable. Employment not only controls the present for the Negro American but, in a most profound way, it is creating the future as well.

For residents of disadvantaged Negro neighborhoods, obtaining good jobs is vastly more difficult than for most workers in society. For decades social, economic, and psychological disadvantages surrounding the urban Negro poor have impaired their work capacities and opportunities.

The result is a cycle of failure: The employment disabilities of one generation breed those of the next.

Unemployment rates for Negroes are double those for whites in every category, including that for married men. This has been true throughout the post–Korean-War period. Moreover, since 1954 unemployment among Negroes has been continuously above the 6 per cent "recession" level widely regarded as a sign of serious economic weakness when prevalent for the entire work force.

Even more important perhaps than unemployment is the related problem of the undesirable nature of many jobs open to Negroes. Negro workers are concentrated in the lowest-skilled and lowest-paying occupations. These jobs often involve substandard wages, great instability and uncertainty of tenure, extremely low status in the eyes of both employer and employee, little or no chance for significant advancement, and unpleasant or exhausting duties. Negro men in particular are more than three times as likely as whites to be in unskilled or service jobs which pay far less than most.

Upgrading the employment of Negro men so that their occupational distribution would be identical with that of the labor force as a whole would have an immense impact upon the nature of their occupations. More than a million nonwhite men would move up the employment ladder into one of the higher-status and higher-paying categories. The effect of such a shift upon the incomes of Negro men would be very great.

Of course, the kind of "instant upgrading" visualized here does not represent a practical alternative for national policy. The economy cannot drastically reduce the total number of low-status jobs it now contains, nor shift large numbers of people upward in occupation in any short period. Therefore, major upgrading in the employment status of Negro men must come through:

1. A faster relative expansion of higher-level jobs than lower-level jobs (which has been occurring for several decades).
2. An improvement in the skills of nonwhite workers, which would enable them to obtain a high proportion of those added better jobs.
3. A drastic reduction of discriminatory hiring and promotion practices in all enterprises, both private and public.

The concentration of male Negro employment at the lowest end of the occupational scale is greatly depressing the incomes of United States Negroes in general. In fact, this is the single most important source of poverty among Negroes. The concentration of Negroes in jobs paying the lowest wages is an even more important source of Negro poverty than is outright unemployment. Potential income gains from upgrading the male Negro labor force are much larger than gains that could be expected from reducing unemployment.

This conclusion underlines the difficulty of improving the economic status of Negro men. It is far easier to create new jobs than it is to create new jobs having relatively high status and earning power. And it is easier to create new jobs than it is to upgrade the employed or partly-employed workers into better-quality employment. Yet only such upgrading will eliminate the fundamental basis of poverty and deprivation among Negro families.

Access to good-quality jobs clearly affects the willingness of Negro men actively to seek work. Of the cities the Commission surveyed, those having the largest proportion of Negroes in skilled and semiskilled work were also the cities having the largest percentage of Negroes active in job-seeking and in participation in the labor force: Negroes were actively engaged to the same extent, or to a greater extent, than were white men. Conversely, in cities where most Negro men were heavily concentrated in menial jobs, they participated less in the labor force than did white men.

Even when given similar employment, Negro workers with the same education as white workers are paid less. This disparity doubtless results to some extent from inferior training in segregated schools, and also from the fact that large numbers of Negroes are only now entering certain occupations for the first time.

However, the differentials are so large and so universal at all educational levels that they clearly reflect the patterns of discrimination which characterize hiring and promotion practices in many segments of the economy.

A higher proportion of Negro women than white women participate in the labor force at nearly all ages except from sixteen to nineteen. The fact that almost half of all adult Negro women are working women reflects the fact that so many Negro males have unsteady and low-paying jobs.

Unemployment rates are, of course, much higher among teen-agers, both Negro and white, than among adults. During the first nine months of 1967 more than one fourth of the Negro teen-agers were unemployed, as compared to one tenth of the white teen-agers.

In disadvantaged areas, employment conditions for Negroes are in a chronic state of crisis. In 1966 the Department of Labor conducted surveys in low-income neighborhoods of nine large cities. These surveys revealed that the rate of Negro unemployment in these cities was about 9 per cent, as compared to about 7 per cent for Negroes generally, and about 3 per cent for whites.

Moreover, a high proportion of the persons living in these areas were "underemployed"; that is, they were either part-time workers looking for full-time employment, or full-time workers earning less than $3000 per year, or they had dropped out of the labor force and were not seeking work. The Department of Labor estimated that the number of people affected by *under*employment is two and one half times greater than the number of *un*employed (those out of work but actively seeking employment) in these areas.

"Subemployment" is a term used to include both the unemployed and the underemployed. The Department of Labor found that the subemployment rate in the nine areas surveyed was nearly nine times greater than the overall unemployment rate for all United States workers.

The critical problem for the Commission was to determine the actual number of those who were unemployed and underemployed in central-city ghettos. Using a process of calculation which is detailed on page 131 of the Government Printing Office edition of the Report, the Commission arrived at the following estimates: the total number of unemployed nonwhite men, women, and teen-agers in central city ghettos was 318,000; the total number of underemployed was 716,000; thus the total number of subemployed was 1,034,000.

Therefore, in order to bring subemployment in these areas down to a level equal to unemployment alone among whites, enough steady, reasonably-paying jobs (and the training and motivation to perform them) must be provided to eliminate all underemployment and reduce unemployment by 65 per cent. The job deficit, for men, women, and teen-agers combined, amounted to 923,000 jobs in 1967.

The chronic unemployment problems in the central city, aggravated by the constant arrival of new unemployed migrants, is the fundamental cause of the persistent poverty in disadvantaged Negro areas.

"Poverty" in the affluent society need not mean absolute privation. Many of the poor in the United States would be well off in other societies.

Relative deprivation—inequality—is a more useful concept of poverty with respect to the Negro in America because it encompasses social and political exclusion as well as economic inequality.

Because of a lack of data on relative deprivation, or inequality, we have had to focus our analysis on a measure of poverty which is both economic and absolute—the Social Security Administration's "poverty level" ($3335 per year for an urban family of four) concept. It is clear, however, that broader measures of poverty would substantiate the conclusions that follow.

In 1966 about 15 per cent of the nation's population had incomes below the "poverty level," as defined by the Social Security Administration.

Of these, over 68 per cent were white (more than twenty million); over 31 per cent were nonwhite (more than nine million).

About 12 per cent of the nation's whites were poor. About 40.6 per cent of the nation's nonwhites were poor.

Over 23 per cent of the nation's poor whites lived in central cities. Close to 42 per cent of the nation's poor nonwhites lived in central cities.

The following facts concerning poverty are relevant to an understanding of the problems faced by people living in disadvantaged neighborhoods. (Source: Social Security Administration, based on 1964 data.)

In central cities about 31 per cent of nonwhite families of two or more persons lived in poverty compared to only about 9 per cent of whites.

Of the ten million poor persons in central cities in 1964, poor whites were much older on the average than poor nonwhites. About 23 per cent of the whites were sixty-five years old or older; but less than 7 per cent of the nonwhites were that old.

Poverty was more than twice as prevalent among nonwhite families with female heads than among those with male heads. In central cities 26 per cent of all nonwhite families of two or more persons were headed by females, as compared to 12 per cent of white families.

Among nonwhite families headed by a female and having children under six years of age, the incidence of poverty was 81 per cent—or over 9 per cent of all nonwhite families in central cities.

The number of poor nonwhite children equalled or surpassed the number of poor white children in every age group.

Two stark facts emerge:

Fifty-four per cent of all poor children in central cities in 1964 were nonwhites.

Of the almost 4.5 million nonwhites living in poverty within central cities, 52 per cent were children under sixteen and 61 per cent were under twenty-one years of age.

The high rates of unemployment and underemployment in racial ghettos are evidence, in part, that many men living in these areas are seeking but cannot obtain jobs which will support a family. Perhaps equally important, most jobs they can get are at the low end of the occupational scale, and often lack the necessary status to sustain a worker's self-respect or the respect of his family and friends. These same men are also constantly confronted with the message of discrimination: "You are inferior because of a trait you did not cause and cannot change." This message reinforces feelings of inadequacy arising from repeated failure to obtain and keep decent jobs.

Wives of these men are forced to go to work, and usually can earn more money than their husbands. If the men stay at home without working, their inadequacies constantly confront them. Tensions arise between them and their wives and children. Under these pressures, it is not surprising that many of these men flee their responsibilities as husbands and fathers. They leave home and drift from city to city, or they adopt the style of "street corner men," spending their days in talk and idleness.

Statistical evidence tends to document this. A close correlation exists between the number of nonwhite married women separated from their husbands each year and the unemployment rate among nonwhite males twenty years old and over.

The impact of marital status on employment among Negroes is shown by the fact that in 1967 the proportion of married men who were either divorced or separated from their wives was more than twice as high among unemployed nonwhite men as among employed nonwhite men. Moreover, among those participating in the labor force, there was a higher proportion of married men with wives present than with wives absent.

The abandonment of the home by many Negro males affects a great many children growing up in the racial ghetto. While most American Negro families are headed by men, just as are most other American families, the proportion of families with female heads is much greater among Negroes than among whites at all income levels, and has been rising in recent years.

This disparity between white and nonwhite families is far greater among the lowest-income families—those most likely to reside in disadvantaged big-city neighborhoods—than among higher-income families. Among families with incomes under $3000 in 1966, the proportion with female heads was 42 per cent for Negroes, but only 23 per cent for whites. In contrast, among families with incomes of $7000 or more, 8 per cent of Negro families had female heads, as compared to 4 per cent of white families.

The problems of fatherlessness are aggravated by the tendency of Negroes to have large families. The average poor,

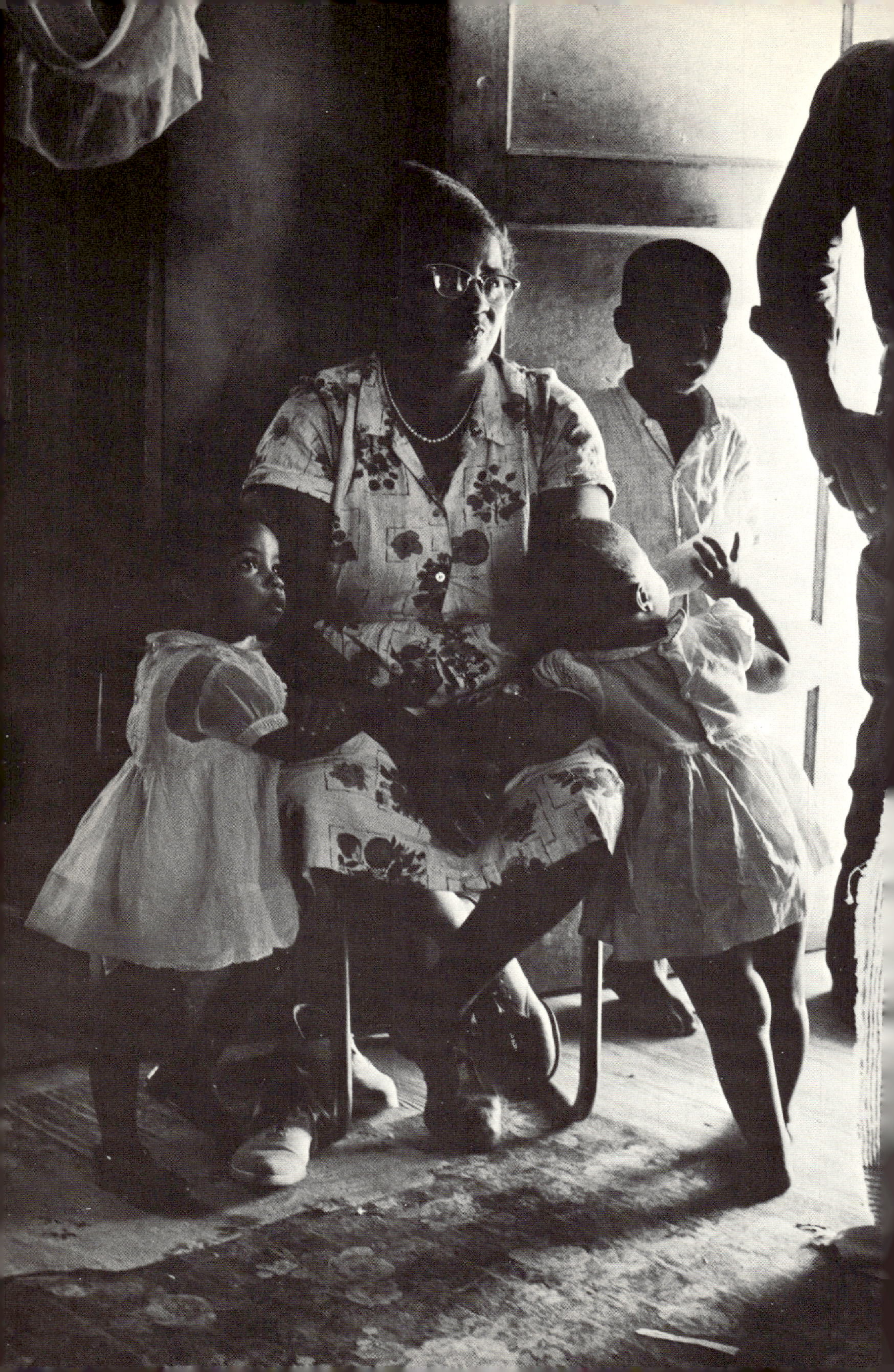

urban, nonwhite family contains 4.8 persons, as compared with 3.7 for the average poor, urban, white family. This is one of the primary factors in the poverty status of nonwhite households in large cities.

The proportion of fatherless families appears to be increasing in the poorest Negro neighborhoods. In the Hough section of Cleveland the proportion of families with female heads rose from 23 to 32 per cent from 1960 to 1965. In the Watts section of Los Angeles it rose from 36 to 39 per cent during the same period.

The handicap imposed on children growing up without fathers, in an atmosphere of poverty and deprivation, is increased because many mothers must work to provide support. With the father absent and the mother working, many ghetto children spend the bulk of their time on the streets. And the streets are those of a crime-ridden, violence-prone, poverty-stricken world.

The image of success in this ghetto world is not that of the "solid citizen," the responsible husband and father, but rather that of the "hustler" who promotes his own interests by exploiting others. The dope sellers and the numbers runners are the "successful" men because their earnings far outstrip those of men who try to climb the economic ladder in honest ways.

Young people in the ghetto are acutely conscious of a system which appears to offer rewards to those who illegally exploit others, and failure to those who struggle under traditional responsibilities. Under these circumstances many adopt exploitation and the "hustle" as a way of life, disclaiming both work and marriage in favor of casual and temporary liaisons. This pattern reinforces itself from one generation to the next, creating a "culture of poverty" and an ingrained cynicism about society and its institutions.

The culture of poverty that results from unemployment and family disorganization generates a system of ruthless, exploitative relationships within the ghetto. Prostitution, dope addiction, casual sexual affairs, and crime create an environmental jungle characterized by personal insecurity and tension. The effects of this development are stark:

The rate of illegitimate births among nonwhite women has risen sharply in the past two decades. In 1940 almost 17 per cent of all nonwhite births were illegitimate; in 1966 over 26 per cent were illegitimate.

The rate of illegitimacy among nonwhite women is closely related to low income and high unemployment rates. In Washington, D.C., for example, an analysis of 1960 census tracts shows that in tracts with unemployment rates of 12 per cent or more among nonwhite men, illegitimacy was over 40 per cent. But in tracts with unemployment rates of 3 per cent and below among nonwhite men, reported illegitimacy was under 20 per cent.

Narcotics addiction is also heavily concentrated in low-income Negro neighborhoods, particularly in New York City. Of the 59,720 addicts known to the United States Bureau of Narcotics at the end of 1966, just over 50 per cent were Negroes.

Not surprisingly, the proportion of nonwhite children who actually attend school (at every age from six through nineteen) is higher for those children who come from homes with both parents present. Children from homes with only one, or neither, parent present do not achieve the attendance record of the former group.

Rates of juvenile delinquency and venereal disease, dependency upon Aid for Dependent Children support, and the use of public assistance in general are much higher in disadvantaged Negro areas than in other parts of large cities.

In conclusion: In 1965, 1.2 million nonwhite children under sixteen lived in central city families headed by a woman under sixty-five years of age. The great majority of these children were growing up in poverty, under conditions that made them better candidates for crime and civil disorder than for jobs providing an entry into American society.

Because of the immense importance of this fact, and because of the potential loss to the society of these young people, we describe these conditions in the following pages.

Life in the Racial Ghetto

The conditions of life in the racial ghetto are strikingly different from those to which most Americans are accustomed —especially white middle-class Americans. We believe it important to describe these conditions and their effect on the lives of people who cannot escape from the ghetto.

Nothing is more fundamental to the quality of life in any area than the sense of personal security of its residents, and nothing affects this sense of security more than crime. In general, crime rates in large cities are much higher than in other areas of our country. Within such cities crime rates are higher in disadvantaged Negro areas than anywhere else.

The most widely used measure of crime is the number of "index crimes" (homicide, forcible rape, aggravated assault, robbery, burglary, grand larceny, and auto theft) in relation to population. In 1966, 1754 such crimes were reported to police for every 100,000 Americans. In cities of over 250,000 the crime rate was close to double the national average, the largest cities having the highest rates. In suburban areas alone, including suburban cities, the rate was only about one third the rate of the largest cities.

Within larger cities, personal and property insecurity has consistently been highest in the older neighborhoods encircling the downtown business district. In most cities, crime rates for many decades have been higher in these inner areas than anywhere else, except in the downtown areas themselves. There, crime rates per 100,000 persons are inflated because of the small number of residents in downtown districts.

High crime rates have persisted in areas encircling the business district even though the ethnic character of their residents has continually changed. Poor immigrants used these areas as "entry ports," then usually moved on to more desirable neighborhoods as soon as they acquired enough resources. Many "entry port" areas have now become racial ghettos.

The difference between crime rates in these disadvantaged neighborhoods and in other parts of the city is usually startling, as a comparison of crime rates in five police districts in Chicago for 1965 illustrates. The data from this study showed that serious crimes against persons per 100,000 residents were thirty-five times greater in a very-low-income Negro district than in a high-income white district, while the rate of crime against property was only two and a half times greater. The lower the income in an area, the higher the crime rate there, with low-income Negro areas having significantly higher crime rates than low-income white areas. This reflects the fact that Negroes as a group have lower incomes than poor whites as a group, and it also reveals the high degree of disorganization in Negro poverty areas. Another fact brought out by the study was that although the Chicago Police Department had assigned over three times as many patrolmen per 100,000 residents to the highest-crime areas, crime rates for offenses against both persons and property combined were almost five times greater there than in the lowest-crime area.

Because most middle-class Americans live in neighborhoods similar to the more crime-free district surveyed, they have little comprehension of the sense of insecurity that characterizes the ghetto resident. Moreover, official statistics normally greatly understate actual crime rates because the vast majority of crimes are not reported to the police.

Two facts are crucial to an understanding of the effects of high crime rates in racial ghettos: Most of these crimes are committed by a small minority of the residents, and the principal victims are the residents themselves. Throughout the United States the great majority of crimes committed by Negroes involve Negro victims.

The majority of law-abiding citizens who live in disadvantaged Negro areas face much higher probabilities of being victimized than do residents of most higher-income areas, including almost all suburbs. For nonwhites the probability of suffering from any index crime except larceny is 78 per cent higher than for whites. The probability of being raped is almost four times higher among nonwhite women than among white women. The probability of being robbed is three and a half times higher for nonwhites in general.

The problems associated with high crime rates generate widespread hostility toward the police in these neighborhoods. Thus, crime not only creates an atmosphere of insecurity and fear throughout Negro neighborhoods, but also causes continuing attrition of the relationship between Negro residents and police. This has a direct bearing on civil disorder.

There are reasons to expect the crime situation in these areas to become worse in the future. First, crime rates throughout the United States have been rising in recent years. Of course, the problem of interpreting and evaluating "rising" crime rates is complicated by the changing age distribution of the population, improvements in reporting methods, and the increasing willingness of victims to report crimes. Despite these complications, there is general agreement on the serious increase in the incidence of crime in the United States.

Crime studies reveal that the rate of index crimes against persons rose 37 per cent from 1960 to 1966 and that the rate of index crimes against property rose 50 per cent. But the number of police available to combat crime is rising much more slowly than the number of crimes, and in spite of significant improvements in police efficiency, it is clear that police will be unable to cope with their expanding work load unless there is a dramatic increase in the resources allocated by society to this task.

Whites and nonwhites in the fourteen to twenty-four age group are responsible for a disproportionately high share of crimes in all parts of the nation. And, for all index crimes together, the arrest rate for Negroes is about four times higher than for whites. It is estimated that in the years 1966 to 1975 the number of Negroes in this age group will increase rapidly, particularly in the central cities—a 63 per cent rise for the young group as compared to only a 32 per cent rise for the total Negro population of central cities.

The residents of the racial ghetto are significantly less healthy than most other Americans. They suffer from higher mortality rates, higher incidence of major diseases, and lower availability and utilization of medical services. They also experience higher admission rates to mental hospitals. These conditions result from a number of factors.

From the standpoint of health, poverty means deficient diets, lack of medical care, inadequate shelter and clothing, and often lack of awareness of potential health needs. As a result, almost 30 per cent of all persons with family incomes less than $2000 per year suffer from chronic health conditions that adversely affect their employment. Less than 8 per cent of families with incomes of $7000 or more suffer from such chronic health conditions.

Poor families have the greatest need for financial assistance in meeting medical expenses. Only about 34 per cent of families with incomes of less than $2000 per year use health insurance benefits. Among families with incomes of $7000 or more, 90 per cent use these benefits.

It is true that public programs of various kinds have been providing significant financial assistance for medical care in recent years. The biggest contributions were made by the

Old Age Assistance Program and the Medical Assistance for the Aged Program. The enactment of Medicare in 1965 has significantly added to this flow of public assistance for medical aid. However, it is too early to evaluate the effects upon health conditions among the poor.

The ills attendant upon poverty are aggravated for Negroes, as compared to whites, for the simple reason that poverty among Negroes is proportionately so much higher. Of all persons who were poor in the United States in 1966, the proportion of nonwhite poor was almost 41 per cent of all nonwhites. Among whites, almost 12 per cent were poor.

Mortality rates for nonwhite mothers are four times as high as those for white mothers. There has been a sharp decline in such rates since 1940. In that year 774 nonwhite and 320 white mothers died for each 100,000 live births. In 1965 only 84 nonwhite and 21 white mothers died per 100,000 live births—but the relative gap between nonwhites and whites actually increased.

Mortality rates among nonwhite babies are 58 per cent higher than among whites for those under one month old. These rates are almost three times as high among those from one month to one year old. This is true in spite of a large drop in infant mortality rates in both groups since 1940.

To some extent because of infant mortality rates, life expectancy at birth was longer for whites (71 years) than for nonwhites (64.1 years) in 1965. Even in the prime working ages, life expectancy is significantly lower among nonwhites than among whites. In 1965 white persons twenty-five years old could expect to live an average of about 49 more years, whereas twenty-five-year-old nonwhites could expect to live another 43 years.

A fact that also contributes to poorer health conditions in the ghetto is that Negro families with incomes similar to those of whites spend less on medical services and visit medical specialists less often. Data gathered July to December 1962 indicate that nonwhite families in the lower income group (under $2000 per family per year) spent less than half as much per person on medical services as did white families with similar incomes.

Negroes spend less on medical care for several reasons. Negro households generally are larger, requiring greater nonmedical expenses for each household and leaving less money for meeting medical expenses. And lower medical expenditures per person would result even if total medical expenditures per household were the same. In addition, fewer doctors, dentists, and medical facilities are conveniently available to Negroes than to most whites. The reason for this is twofold: the geographic concentration of doctors in higher-income areas in large cities, and discrimination against Negroes by doctors and hospitals. The result is fewer visits to physicians and dentists by people from poor neighborhoods.

Although widespread use of health insurance has led many hospitals to adopt nondiscriminatory policies, some private hospitals still refuse to admit Negro patients or to accept doctors with Negro patients. And many individual doctors still discriminate against Negro patients. As a result, Negroes are more likely to be treated in hospital clinics than are whites, and they are less likely to receive personalized service.

Environmental conditions in disadvantaged Negro neighborhoods create further reasons for poor health conditions there. The level of sanitation is strikingly below that which is prevalent in most higher-income areas. One simple reason is that residents often lack proper storage facilities for food —adequate refrigerators, freezers, even garbage cans, which

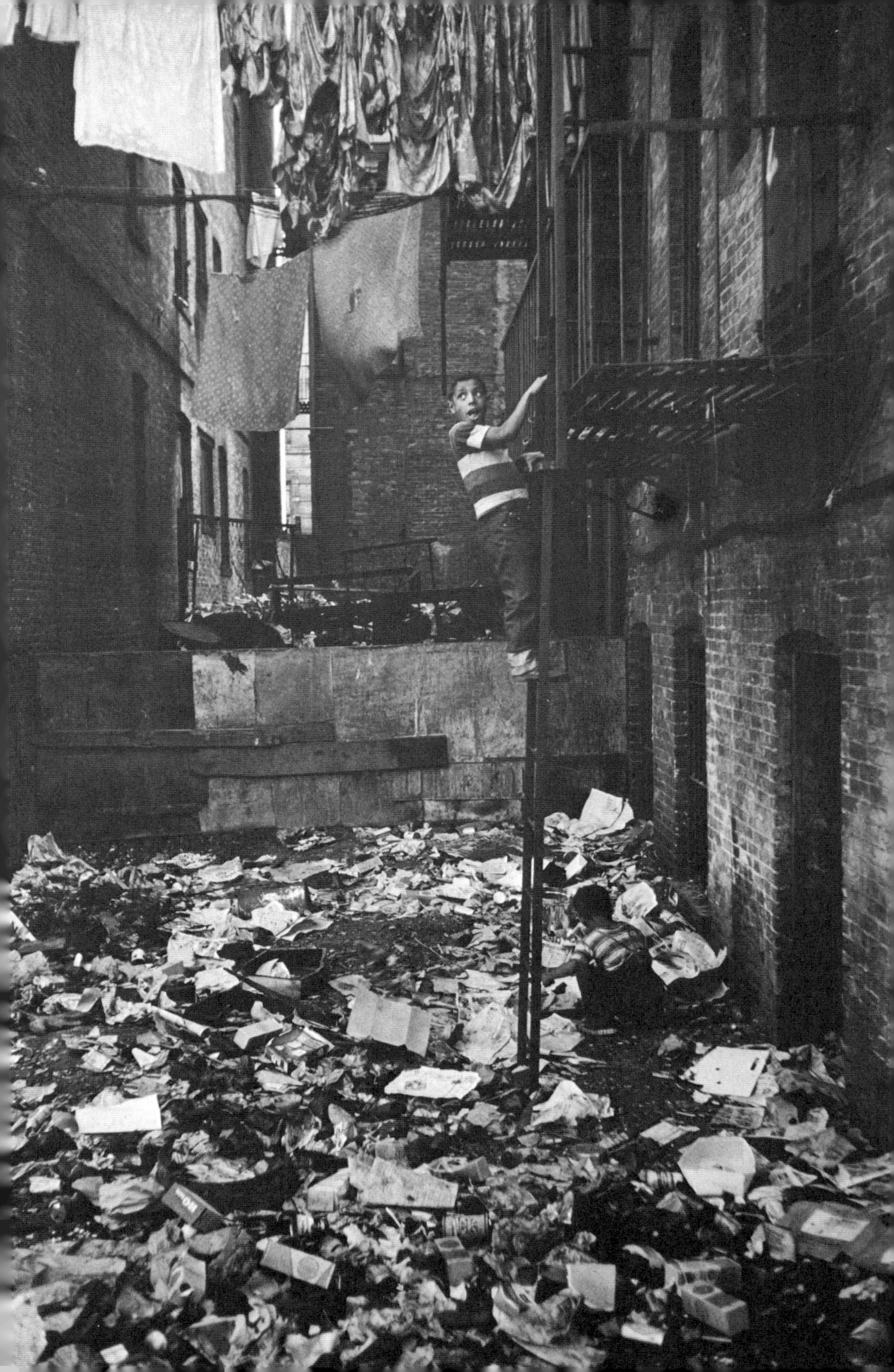

are sometimes stolen as fast as landlords can replace them.

In areas where garbage collection and other sanitation services are grossly inadequate—commonly in the poorer parts of our large cities—rats proliferate. It is estimated that in 1965 there were over fourteen thousand cases of ratbite in the United States, mostly in such neighborhoods. The importance of these conditions was outlined in a memorandum to the Commission dated November 16, 1967, from Robert Patricelli, minority counsel for the Subcommittee on Employment, Manpower, and Poverty, United States Senate:

> Sanitation Commissioners of New York City and Chicago both feel this [sanitation] to be an important community problem and report themselves as being under substantial pressure to improve conditions.
> *It must be concluded that slum sanitation is a serious problem in the minds of the urban poor and well merits, at least on that ground, the attention of the Commission.* A related problem, according to one Sanitation Commissioner, is the fact that residents of areas bordering on slums feel that sanitation and neighborhood cleanliness is a crucial issue, relating to the stability of their blocks and constituting an important psychological index of "how far gone" their area is.
> . . . There is no known study comparing sanitation services between slum and nonslum areas. The experts agree, however, that there are more services in the slums on a quantitative basis, although perhaps not on a per capita basis. In New York City, for example, garbage pickups are supposedly scheduled for about six times a week in slums, compared to three times a week in other areas of the city; the comparable figures in Chicago are two-to-three times a week versus once a week.
> The point, therefore, is not the relative quantitative level of services but the peculiarly intense needs of ghetto areas for sanitation services. This high demand is the product of numerous factors, including: (1) higher population density; (2) lack of well-managed buildings and adequate services provided by landlords, number of receptacles, necessity for carrying refuse to curbside, number of electric garbage disposals; (3) high

relocation rates of tenants and businesses, producing a heavy volume of bulk refuse left on streets and in buildings; (4) different uses of the streets—as outdoor living rooms in summer, recreation areas—where the presence of garbage arouses sensitivity to the problem; (5) large numbers of abandoned cars; (6) severe rodent and pest problems; (7) traffic congestion blocking garbage collection; and (8) obstructed street cleaning and snow removal on crowded, car-choked streets. Each of these elements adds to the problem and suggests a different possible line of attack.

Much of the violence in recent civil disorders has been directed at stores and other commercial establishments in disadvantaged Negro areas. In some cases, rioters focused on stores operated by white merchants who, they apparently believed, had been charging exorbitant prices or selling inferior goods. Not all the violence against these stores can be attributed to "revenge" for such practices. Yet it is clear that many residents of disadvantaged Negro neighborhoods believe they suffer constant abuses by local merchants.

Significant grievances concerning unfair commercial practices affecting Negro consumers were found in eleven of the twenty cities studied by the Commission. The fact that most of the merchants who operate stores in Negro areas are white undoubtedly contributes to the conclusion among Negroes that they are exploited by white society.

It is difficult to assess the precise degree and extent of exploitation. No systematic and reliable survey comparing consumer pricing and credit practices in all-Negro and other neighborhoods has ever been conducted on a nationwide basis.

Differences in prices and credit practices between white middle-income areas and Negro low-income areas to some extent reflect differences in the real costs of serving these two markets. For instance, there are differences in loss through pilferage in supermarkets in different neighborhoods. The exact extent of cost differences has never been estimated accurately. Finally, an examination of exploitative consumer practices must consider the particular structure and functions of the low-income consumer durables market.

This complex situation can best be understood by first considering certain basic facts:

Various cultural factors generate constant pressure on low-income families to buy many relatively expensive durable goods and display them in their homes. This pressure comes in part from continuous exposure to commercial advertising, especially on television. In January 1967 over 88 per cent of all Negro households had TV sets. A 1961 study of 464 low-income families in New York City showed that 95 per cent of these relatively poor families had TV sets.

Many poor families have extremely low incomes, bad credit records, unstable sources of income, or other attributes which make it virtually impossible for them to buy merchandise from large established national or local retail firms. These families lack enough savings to pay cash, and they cannot meet the standard credit requirements of established general merchants because they are too likely to fall behind in their payments.

Poor families in urban areas are far less mobile than others. A 1967 Chicago study of low-income Negro households indicated that their low automobile ownership compelled them to patronize neighborhood merchants. These merchants typically provided smaller selections and poorer services, and charged higher prices than big national outlets.

Most low-income families are uneducated concerning the nature of credit-purchase contracts, the legal rights and obligations of both buyers and sellers, the sources of advice for consumers who are having difficulties with merchants, and the operation of the courts concerned with these matters. In contrast, merchants engaged in selling goods to them are very well informed.

In most states, the laws governing relations between consumers and merchants *in effect* offer protection only to informed, sophisticated parties who have an understanding of each other's rights and obligations. Consequently, these laws are little suited to protecting the rights of most low-income consumers.

In this situation, exploitative practices flourish. Ghetto residents who want to buy relatively expensive goods cannot do so from standard retail outlets and are thus restricted to local stores. Forced to use credit, they have little understanding of the pitfalls of credit buying. But because they have unstable incomes and frequently fail to make payments, the cost to the merchants of serving them is significantly above that of serving middle-income consumers. Consequently, a special kind of merchant appears, to sell them goods on terms designed to cover the high cost of doing business in ghetto neighborhoods.

Whether or not they actually gain higher profits, these merchants charge higher prices than those in other parts of the city. They set higher prices in order to cover the greater credit risks and other higher operating costs inherent in neighborhood outlets. A recent study conducted by the Federal Trade Commission in Washington, D.C., illustrates this conclusion dramatically. The FTC identified a number of stores specializing in selling furniture and appliances to low-income households.

About 92 per cent of the sales of these stores were credit sales involving installment purchases, as compared to 27 per cent of the sales in general retail outlets handling the same merchandise.

The median annual income of a sample of 486 customers of these stores was about $4200. But one third had annual incomes below $3600; about 6 per cent were receiving welfare payments; and another 76 per cent were employed in

USE OUR **LAY AWAY** OR EASY PAYMENT **PLAN**

"BIG" T.V. DISCOUNT

SHOWROOM

SYLVANIA Radios
A Gift Worth Giving

WESTINGHOUSE SPECIAL
$15.95
1.95 DISC.
$14.00
STEAM IRON

the lowest-paying occupations (service workers, operatives, laborers, and domestics).

Definitely catering to a low-income group, these stores charged significantly higher prices than general merchandise outlets in the Washington area. According to testimony by Paul Rand Dixon, Chairman of the FTC, an item selling wholesale at $100 would retail on the average for $165 in a general merchandise store and for $250 in a low-income specialty store. Thus, the customers of these outlets were paying an average premium of about 52 per cent.

Higher prices are not necessarily exploitative in themselves. But many merchants in ghetto neighborhoods take advantage of their superior knowledge of credit buying by engaging in various exploitative tactics—high pressure salesmanship, "bait advertising," misrepresentation of prices, substitution of used goods for promised new ones, failure to notify consumers of legal actions against them, refusal to repair or replace substandard goods, exorbitant prices or credit charges, and use of shoddy merchandise. Such tactics affect a great many low-income consumers.

In the 1961 New York study cited on p. 170, 60 per cent of the low-income households had suffered from consumer problems (some of which were purely their own fault). About 23 per cent had experienced serious exploitation. Another 20 per cent, many of whom were also exploited, had experienced repossession, garnishment, or threat of garnishment.

Garnishment practices in many states allow creditors to deprive individuals of their wages through court action, without a hearing or trial.

In about twenty states, the wages of an employee can be diverted to a creditor merely upon the latter's deposition, with no advance hearing at which the employee can defend himself. He often receives no prior notice of such action and is usually unaware of the law's operation, and too poor to hire legal defense.

Moreover, consumers may find themselves still owing money on a sales contract even after the creditor has repossessed the goods. The New York study indicated that 10 per cent of a sample of low-income families had been subjected to legal action regarding consumer purchases. And the Federal Trade Commission study in Washington, D.C., showed that, on the average, retailers specializing in credit sales of furniture and appliances to low-income consumers resorted to court action once for every $2200 of sales. Since their average sale was for $207, this amounted to using the courts to collect from one of every eleven customers.

In contrast, department stores in the same area used court action against approximately one of every 14,500 customers (assuming their sales also averaged $207 per customer).

Residents of low-income Negro neighborhoods frequently claim that they pay higher prices for food in local markets than wealthier white suburbanites, and that they receive inferior quality meat and produce.

Statistically reliable information comparing prices and quality in these two kinds of areas is generally unavailable. The United States Bureau of Labor Statistics, studying food prices in six cities in 1966, compared prices of a standard list of eighteen items in low-income areas and higher-income areas in each city. In a total of 180 stores, including independent and chain stores, and for items of the same type sold in the same types of stores, there were no significant differences in prices between low-income and high-income areas.

However, stores in low-income areas were more likely to

be small independents (which had somewhat higher prices). They were more likely to sell low-quality produce and meat at any given price, and to be patronized by people who typically bought smaller-sized packages, which are more expensive per unit measure. In other words, many low-income consumers in fact pay higher prices, although the situation varies greatly from place to place.

Although these findings must be considered inconclusive, there are significant reasons to believe that poor households generally pay higher prices for the food they buy, and that they receive food of lower quality. Low-income consumers buy more food at local groceries because they are less mobile. Prices in these small stores are significantly higher than in major supermarkets because they cannot achieve economies of scale, and because real operating costs are higher in low-income Negro areas than in outlying suburbs. For instance, inventory "shrinkage" from pilfering and other causes is normally under 2 per cent of sales, but can run twice as much in high-crime areas. Managers seek to make up for these added costs by charging higher prices for food or by substituting lower grades.

These practices do not necessarily involve exploitation, but they are often perceived as exploitative and unfair by those who are aware of the price and quality differences involved, but unaware of operating costs. In addition, it is probable that genuinely exploitative pricing practices exist in some areas. In either case, differential food prices constitute another factor which convinces urban Negroes in low-income neighborhoods that whites discriminate against them.

"We" Made It, Why Can't "They"?

In the preceding pages we have surveyed the historical background of racial discrimination and traced its effects on Negro employment, on the social structure of the ghetto community, and on the conditions of life that surround the urban Negro poor. Here we address a fundamental question which many white Americans are asking today: Why has the Negro been unable to escape from poverty and the ghetto? The European immigrants "made it"—why can't the Negro?

The changing nature of the American economy is one major reason for the Negro's inability to move up and out of the ghetto.

When the European immigrants were arriving in large numbers, America was becoming an urban-industrial society. To build its major cities and industries, America needed great pools of unskilled labor. The immigrants provided the labor, gained an economic foothold, and thereby enabled their children and grandchildren to move up to skilled, white-collar, and professional employment.

Since World War II, especially, America's urban-industrial society has matured; unskilled labor is far less essential than before, and blue-collar jobs of all kinds are decreasing in number and importance as a source of new employment. The Negroes who migrated to the great urban centers after World War II lacked the skills essential to the new economy, and the schools of the ghetto have been unable to provide the education that could qualify them for decent jobs. The Negro migrant, unlike the immigrant, found little opportunity in the city. He had arrived too late. The unskilled labor he had to offer was no longer needed.

Racial discrimination is undoubtedly the second major reason why the Negro has been unable to escape from poverty. The structure of discrimination has persistently narrowed his opportunities and restricted his prospects. Well before the high tide of immigration to America from overseas, Negro Americans were already relegated to the poorly-paid, low-status occupations in their homeland.

Had it not been for racial discrimination, the North might well have recruited Southern Negroes after the Civil War to provide the labor for building the burgeoning urban-industrial economy. Instead, Northern employers looked to Europe for their sources of unskilled labor. Upon the arrival of the immigrants, the Negroes were dislodged from the few occupations they had dominated. Not until World War II were Negroes generally hired for industrial jobs, and by that time the decline in the need for unskilled labor had already begun. European immigrants, too, suffered from discrimination, but never was it so pervasive. The prejudice against color in America has formed a bar to advancement unlike any other.

Political opportunities also played an important role in enabling the European immigrants to escape from poverty. The immigrants settled, for the most part, in rapidly growing cities that had powerful and expanding political machines. These machines gave them economic advantages in exchange for political support.

The political machines were decentralized, which meant that ward-level grievance machinery, as well as personal representation, made it possible for the immigrant to make his voice heard and his power felt. Since the local political organizations exercised considerable influence over public building in the cities, they were able to provide employment in construction jobs for their immigrant voters. Ethnic groups often dominated one or more of the municipal services—police and fire protection, sanitation, and even public education.

The Irish and other immigrants were given jobs by the political machines in exchange for party loyalty.

By the time the Negroes arrived in the industrial cities, the situation had altered dramatically. The great wave of public building had virtually come to an end. Reform groups were beginning to attack the political machines. The machines were no longer so powerful, nor were they so well equipped to provide jobs and other favors.

Political machines retained their hold over the areas settled by Negroes, but the scarcity of patronage jobs made machine politicians unwilling to share with Negroes the political positions they had created in those neighborhoods. For example, Harlem was dominated by white politicians for many years after it had become a Negro ghetto. Even today, New York's Lower East Side, which is now predominantly Puerto Rican, is strongly influenced by politicians of the older immigrant groups.

This pattern exists in many other American cities. Negroes are still underrepresented in city councils and in most city agencies.

Segregation played a role here, too. The immigrants and their descendants, who felt threatened by the arrival of the Negro, prevented a Negro-immigrant coalition that might have saved the old political machines. Moreover, the reform groups, nominally more liberal on the race issue than the machines, were often dominated by businessmen and middle-class city residents who usually opposed coalition with any low-income group, white or black.

Cultural factors also made it easier for the immigrants to escape from poverty. They came to America from much poorer societies, where the standard of living was low. And they came at a time when most jobs in the American economy were unskilled. They sensed little deprivation in being forced to take the dirty and poorly-paid jobs. Also, their families were large; many breadwinners, some of whom never married, contributed to the total family income.

These family units managed to live on the incomes from even the lowest-paid jobs and still put some money aside for savings or investment; for example, to purchase a house or tenement, or to open a store or factory. Since the immigrants spoke little English and had their own ethnic culture, they needed stores to supply them with ethnic foods and other services. Since their family structures were patriarchal, men found satisfactions in family life that helped compensate for the bad jobs they had to take and the hard work they had to endure.

Negroes came to the city under quite different circumstances. They were generally relegated to jobs that others would not take, and they were paid too little to be able to put money in savings for new enterprises.

In addition, Negroes lacked the extended family characteristic of certain European groups; each household usually had only one or two breadwinners. Moreover, Negro men had fewer cultural incentives to work in a dirty job for the sake of the family. As a result of slavery and of long periods of male unemployment afterward, the Negro family structure had become matriarchal. The man played a secondary and marginal role in his family. For many Negro men, then, there were few of the cultural and psychological rewards of family life. They often abandoned their homes because they felt themselves useless to their families.

Although Negro men worked as hard as the immigrants to support their families, their rewards were not as great. The jobs did not pay enough to enable them to make a good living because prices and living standards had risen since the immigrants had come, and the business opportunities that had allowed some immigrants to become independent, even rich, had vanished.

But above all, Negroes suffered from segregation. Segregation denied them access to the good jobs and the effective unions. Segregation deprived them of the opportunity to buy real estate or obtain business loans or move out of the ghetto and bring up their children in middle-class neighborhoods. Immigrants were able to leave their ghettos as soon as they had money; segregation has denied Negroes the opportunity to live elsewhere.

Finally, nostalgia makes it easy to exaggerate the ease of escape of the white immigrants from the ghettos. When the immigrants were immersed in poverty, they, too, lived in slums, and their neighborhoods exhibited fearfully high rates of alcoholism, desertion, illegitimacy, and other pathologies associated with poverty. Just as some Negro men desert their families when they are unemployed and their wives can get jobs, so did the men of other ethnic groups—even though time and affluence has clouded white memories of the past.

Today whites tend to contrast their experience with that of poverty-stricken Negroes. The fact is, among the southern and eastern Europeans who came to America in the last great wave of immigration, those who came *already urbanized* were the first to escape from poverty.

The others, who came to America from rural backgrounds, as Negroes did, are only now, after three generations, in the final stages of escaping from poverty. Until the last ten years or so, most of these were employed in blue-collar jobs, and only a small proportion of their children were able or willing to attend college. In other words, only the third—and in many cases only the fourth—generation has been able to achieve the kind of middle-class income and status that allows it to send its children to college. Because of favorable economic and political conditions, these ethnic groups were able to escape from lower-class status to working-class and lower-middle-income status. But it has taken them three generations.

A slum street on New York's lower east side in the early 1900's

Negroes have been concentrated in the city for only two generations, and they have been there under far less favorable conditions than those faced earlier by European ethnic groups. Moreover, their escape from poverty has been blocked in part by the resistance of the European ethnic groups. They have been unable to enter some unions and to move into some neighborhoods outside the ghetto because descendants of the European immigrants who control these unions and neighborhoods have not yet abandoned them for middle-class occupations and areas.

Even so, some Negroes have escaped poverty, and they have done so in only two generations. Their success is less visible than that of the immigrants in many cases, for residential segregation has forced them to remain in the ghetto. Still, the proportion of nonwhites employed in white-collar, technical, and professional jobs has risen from slightly over 10 per cent in 1950 to almost 21 per cent in 1966, and the proportion attending college has risen an equal amount. Indeed, the development of a small but steadily increasing Negro middle class, while a great part of the Negro population is stagnating economically, is creating a growing gap between Negro haves and have-nots.

The awareness of this gap on the part of those left behind undoubtedly adds to the feelings of desperation and anger which breed civil disorders. Low-income Negroes realize that segregation and lack of job opportunities have made it possible for only a small proportion of all Negroes to escape poverty, and the summer disorders are at least in part a protest against being left behind and left out.

The immigrant who labored long hours at hard and often menial work had the hope of a better future, if not for himself, then for his children. This was the promise of "the American dream." The society offered to all a future that was open-ended; with hard work and perseverance, a man and his family could in time achieve not only material well-being but "position" and status.

For the Negro family in the urban ghetto there is a different vision—the future seems to lead only to a dead end.

What the American economy of the late nineteenth and early twentieth century was able to do to help the European immigrants escape from poverty is now largely impossible. New methods of escape must be found for the majority of today's poor.

PART III: WHAT CAN BE DONE?

The Community and the Poor

The racial disorders during the summer of 1967 reflect, in part, the failure at all levels of government—Federal and state as well as local—to come to grips with the problems of our cities. The ghetto symbolizes the dilemma created by a widening gap between human needs and public resources, and a growing cynicism regarding the commitment of community institutions and leadership to meet these needs.

The problem has many dimensions—financial, political, and institutional. Almost all cities, and particularly the central cities of the largest metropolitan regions, are simply unable to meet the growing need for public services and facilities with the funds that can be raised from traditional sources of municipal revenue. Many cities are structured politically in such a way that great numbers of citizens, particularly minority groups, have little or no representation in the processes of government. Finally, some cities lack either the will or the capacity to use effectively the resources that are available to them.

Instrumentalities of Federal and state government often compound the problems. National policy, expressed through a very large number of grant programs and institutions, rarely exhibits a coherent and consistent perspective when view at the local level. State efforts, traditionally focused on rural areas, often fail to tie in effectively with either local or Federal programs in urban areas.

Meanwhile, the decay of the central city continues. The revenue base of the central city has been eroded by the retreat of industry and of middle-class families to the suburbs. Its budget and tax rate have been inflated by rising costs and increasing numbers of dependent citizens. And its public plant—schools, hospitals, and correctional institutions—has deteriorated because of age and long-deferred maintenance.

Yet, to most citizens the decay remains largely invisible. Only their tax bills, and the headlines they read concerning crime or "riots," suggest that something may be seriously wrong with the city.

There are, however, two groups of people that live constantly with the problem of the city: public officials and the poor, particularly poor residents of the racial ghetto. The relationship of these two groups is a key factor in the development of conditions underlying civil disorders.

Our investigations of the 1967 riot cities establish that:

> Virtually every major episode of urban violence in the summer of 1967 was foreshadowed by an accumulation of the unresolved grievances of ghetto residents against local authorities (often, but not always, the police). So high was the resulting underlying tension that routine and random events, tolerated or ignored under most circumstances (such as the raid on the "blind pig" in Detroit), became the triggers of sudden violence.
>
> Not only was there a high level of dissatisfaction, but confidence in the willingness and ability of local government to respond to Negro grievances was low. Evidence presented to this Commission in hearings, field reports, and research analyses of the 1967 riot cities establishes that a substantial number of Negroes were disturbed and angry about local governments' failures to solve their problems.

Several developments have converged to produce this volatile situation.

First, there is a widening gulf in communications between local government and the residents of the erupting ghettos of the city. As a result, many Negro citizens develop a profound sense of isolation and alienation from the processes and programs of government. Although all residents of our larger cities experience this lack of communication, it is

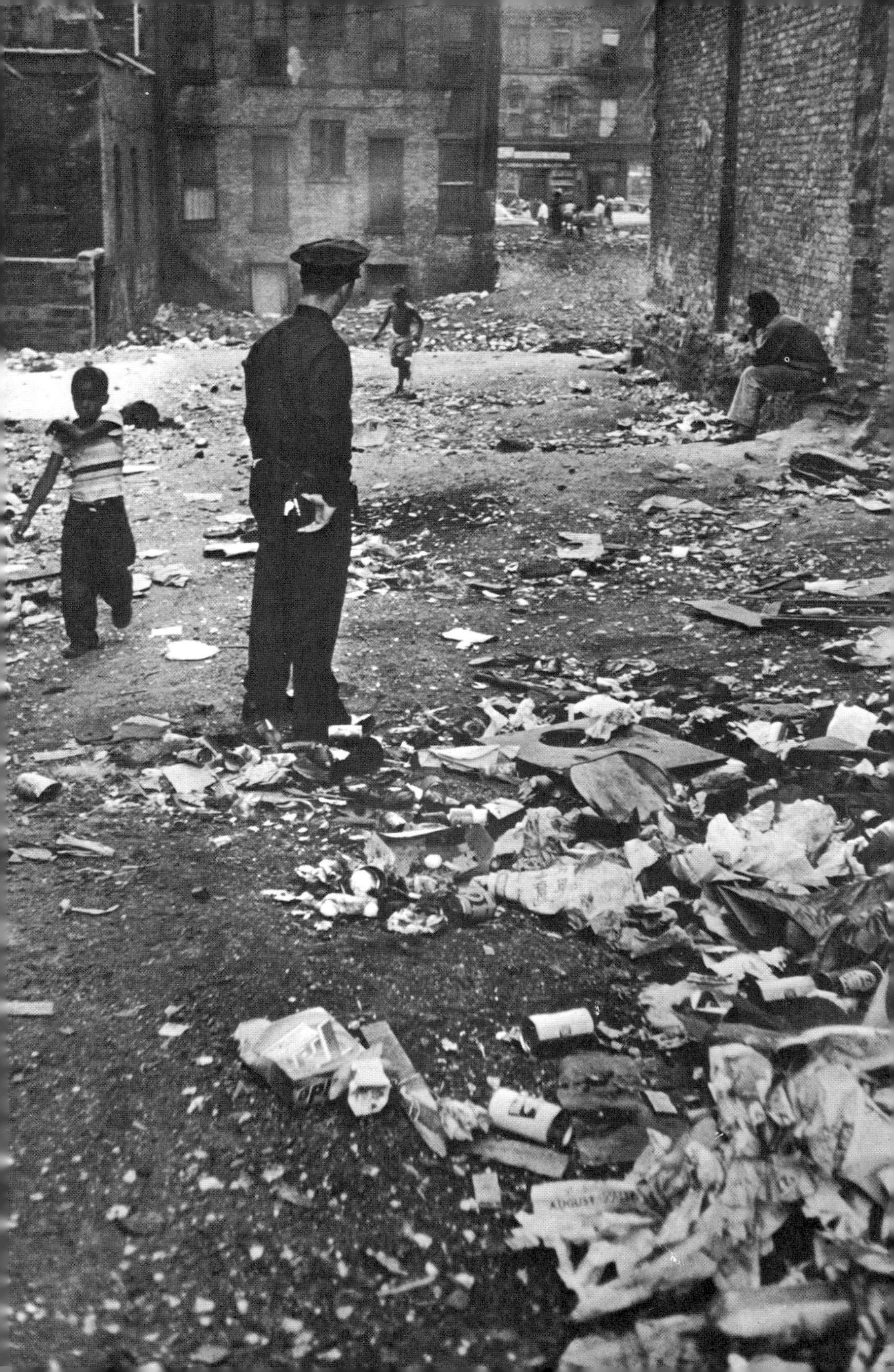

much more difficult for the low-income, poorly-educated citizens to overcome. And because the poor are disproportionately supported by and dependent upon programs administered by agencies of local government, it is they who more often are subject to real or imagined official discourtesy, seeming disinterest, or arbitrary administrative actions.

Further, as a result of the long history of racial discrimination, the grievances of Negroes often take on personal and symbolic significance transcending the immediate consequences of a particular event. For example, inadequate sanitation services are viewed by many ghetto residents as not merely instances of poor public service but as manifestations of racial discrimination. This perception reinforces existing feelings of alienation and contributes to a heightened level of frustration and dissatisfaction, not only with the administrators of the sanitation department but with all the representatives of local government. This is particularly true with respect to the police, who are the only public agents on duty in the ghetto twenty-four hours a day, and who bear the burden of a hostility toward the less visible elements of the system.

The lack of communication and the absence of regular contacts with ghetto residents prevent city leaders from learning about problems and grievances as they develop. As a result, tensions which could have been dissipated if responded to promptly mount unnecessarily, and the potential for explosion grows inevitably. And once disorder erupts, public officials are frequently unable to fashion an effective response. They lack adequate information about the nature of the trouble and its causes, and they lack rapport with local leaders who might be able to influence the community.

Second, many city governments are poorly organized to respond effectively to the needs of ghetto residents, even when those needs are made known to appropriate public officials.

Most middle-class city dwellers have limited contacts with local government. When contacts do occur, they tend to concern relatively narrow and specific problems. Furthermore, middle-class citizens, although subject to many of the same frustrations and resentments as ghetto residents in dealing with the public bureaucracy, find it relatively easy to locate the appropriate agency for help and redress. If they fail to get satisfaction, they can ask for the assistance of elected representatives, friends in government, or a lawyer. In short, the middle-class city dweller has relatively fewer needs for public services and is reasonably well positioned to move the system to his benefit.

On the other hand, the typical ghetto resident has interrelated social and economic problems which require the services of several government and private agencies. At the same time, he may be unable to identify his problems in terms of the complicated structure of government. Moreover, he may be unaware of his rights and opportunities under public programs and unable to obtain the necessary guidance from either public or private sources.

Current trends in municipal administration have had the effect of reducing the capacity of local government to respond effectively to these problems. The pressures for administrative efficiency and cost cutting have brought about the withdrawal of many operations of city government from direct contact with neighborhood and citizen. Red tape and administrative complexity have filled the vacuum created by the centralization of local government. The introduction of a merit system and a professionalized civil service has made management of the cities more business-like, but it has

A meeting between city planners and area residents

also tended to depersonalize and isolate government. And the rigid patterns of segregation prevalent within the central city have widened the distance between Negro citizens and the city hall.

In most of the riot cities surveyed by the Commission we found little or no meaningful coordination among city agencies, either in responding to the needs of ghetto residents on an ongoing basis or in planning to head off disturbances. The consequences of this lack of coordination were particularly severe for the police. Despite the fact that they were being called upon increasingly to deal with tensions and citizen complaints that often had little, if anything, to do with police services, the police departments of many large cities were isolated from other city agencies. Sometimes they were isolated even from the mayor and his staff. In these cities, the police were compelled to deal with ghetto residents angered over dirty streets, dilapidated housing, unfair commercial practices, or inferior schools—grievances which they had neither the responsibility for creating nor the authority to redress.

Third, ghetto residents increasingly believe that they are excluded from the decision-making process which affects their lives and community. This feeling of exclusion, intensified by the bitter legacy of racial discrimination, has engendered a deep-seated hostility toward the institutions of government. It has severely compromised the effectiveness of programs intended to provide improved services to ghetto residents.

In part, this is the lesson of Detroit, where well intentioned programs, designed to respond to the needs of ghetto residents, were not worked out and implemented sufficiently in cooperation with the people who were supposed to benefit from the programs. A report prepared for the Senate Subcommittee on Employment, Manpower, and Poverty, presented just prior to the riot in Detroit, found that:

> Area residents . . . complain almost continually that their demands for program changes are not heeded, that they have little voice in what goes on. . . . As much as the area residents are involved, listened to, and even heeded . . . it becomes fairly clear that the relationship is still one of superordinate-subordinate, rather than one of equals. . . . The procedures by which HRD (the Mayor's Committee for Human Resources Development, the Detroit Community Action Agency) operates generally admit the contributions of area residents only after programs have been written; after policies have already operated for a time or have already been formulated; and to a large degree, only in formal and infrequent meetings rather than in day-to-day operations. . . . The meaningfulness of resident involvement is reduced by its after-the-fact nature and by the relatively limited resources residents have at their disposal.

Mayor Alfonso J. Cervantes of St. Louis was even more explicit. In testimony before this Commission he stated:

> We have found that ghetto neighborhoods cannot be operated on from outside alone. The people within them should have a voice, and our experience has shown that it is often a voice that speaks with good sense, since the practical aspect of the needs of the ghetto people are so much clearer to the people there than they are to anyone else.

The political system, traditionally an important vehicle for the effective participation of minorities in decisions affecting the distribution of public resources, has not worked for the Negro as it has for other groups. The reasons are fairly obvious.

We have found that the number of Negro officials in elected and appointed positions in the riot cities is minimal in proportion to the Negro population. The alienation of the Negro from the political process has been exacerbated by his racial and economic isolation.

Specifically, the needs of ghetto residents for social welfare and other public services have swelled dramatically at a time when increased affluence has diminished the need of the rest of the urban population for such services. By reducing disproportionately the economic disability of other portions of the population, particularly other ethnic urban minorities, this affluence has left the urban Negro few potential local allies with whom to make common cause for shared objectives. The development of political alliances, essential to effective participation of minority groups in the political process, has been further impaired by the polarization of the races, which on both sides has transformed economic considerations into racial issues.

Finally, these developments have coincided with the demise of the historic urban political machines and the growth of the city-manager concept of government (according to which the city manager is not publicly elected but appointed by the city council). While this tendency has produced major benefits in terms of honest and efficient administration, it has eliminated an important political link between city government and low-income residents.

These conditions have produced a vast and threatening disparity in perceptions of the intensity and validity of Negro dissatisfaction. Viewed from the perspective of the ghetto resident, city government appears distant and unconcerned, the possibility of effective change remote. As a result, tension rises perceptibly; the explosion comes as the climax to a progression of tension-generating incidents. To the city administration, unaware of this growing tension or unable to respond effectively to it, the outbreak of disorder comes as a shock.

No democratic society can long endure the existence within

its major urban centers of a substantial number of citizens who feel deeply aggrieved as a group, yet lack confidence that the government will rectify perceived injustice, and confidence in their own ability to bring about needed change.

We are aware that reforms in existing instruments of local government, and reforms in their relationship to the ghetto population, will mean little unless joined with a sincere and comprehensive response to the severe social and economic needs of ghetto residents.

We believe that there are measures which can and should be taken now. They can be put to work without great cost and without delay. They can be built upon in the future. They will effectively reduce the level of grievance and tension as well as improve the responsiveness of local government to the needs of ghetto residents.

It is vital, however, that the first-phase programs not be regarded or perceived as short-term antiriot efforts, as merely today's stop-gap remedies for cooling already inflamed situations. These programs will have little chance of succeeding unless they are part of a long-range commitment to action designed to eliminate the fundamental sources of grievance and tension.

The Commission recommends that six first-phase actions be taken by large cities facing problems of unrest, dissatisfaction, and decay in their central cities.

Develop Neighborhood Action Task Forces The task forces should be made up of representatives of both government and community. The goal would be to achieve more effective communication between government and ghetto residents and to provide an opportunity for effective citizen participation in decision making. The Commission believes that the task-force approach could bring the energies and resources of both city government and the private sector to bear on the real needs and priorities of low-income residents, and that it could do much to generate a new sense of community.

Establish Effective Grievance-Response Mechanisms A grievance agency, separate from operating municipal agencies, should have general jurisdiction in grievances against all public agencies and authorities, and have the authority to investigate and make public its findings and recommendations. The grievance procedure should be easy for ghetto residents to use. It should guarantee that grievants be given full opportunity to take part in all proceedings and be represented by counsel.

Expand Legal Services for the Poor Among the most intense grievances underlying the riots of 1967 were those which derived from conflicts between ghetto residents and private parties, especially white landlords and merchants. Resourceful and imaginative use of available legal processes could contribute significantly to the alleviation of such tensions. But ghetto residents also have need for advocacy in a variety of other contexts. The local bar bears major responsibility for devising ways of bringing increased and more effective legal aid to the poor, such aid to be financed by increased private and public funding.

Provide Assistance for Mayors and City Councils The capacity of the Federal government to affect local problems depends to a great extent on the capacity of city government to respond competently to Federal government program initiatives. Therefore representatives of Federal programs, mayors, and city councils need to create new mechanisms to aid in decision making, program planning, and coordination. Both state and Federal governments should offer financial assistance for developing these new, critically needed mechanisms for cooperative effort.

Sponsor Meetings of Legislative Bodies and Ghetto Residents The city legislative body should hold a series of meetings on ghetto problems—with ghetto residents participating fully—for the purpose of identifying ghetto grievances that can best be addressed by legislative action, and establishing a foundation for needed legislation.

Expand Employment of Ghetto Residents Local government should make a concerted effort to provide substantial employment opportunities for ghetto residents through deliberate employment, training, and upgrading of Negroes. Municipal authorities should review civil-service policies and job standards and take prompt action to remove arbitrary barriers to employment. Employment qualification tests and police records should be given careful re-evaluation. Local government action in this vital area could stimulate private employers to take similar action.

Finally, there remains the issue of leadership. Now, as never before, the American city has need for the personal qualities of strong democratic leadership. Given the difficulties and delays involved in administrative reorganization or institutional change, the best hope for the city in the short run lies in this powerful instrument. In most cities, the mayor will have the prime responsibility.

It is in large part his role now to create a sense of commitment and concern for the problems of the ghetto community and to set the tone for the entire relationship between the institutions of city government and all the citizenry.

Part of the task is to interpret the problems of the ghetto community to the citizenry at large and to generate channels of communication between Negro and white leadership outside of government. Only if all the institutions of the community—those outside the government as well as those inside the structure—are implicated in the problems of the ghetto can the alienation and distrust of disadvantaged citizens be overcome.

This is now the decisive role of the urban mayor. As leader and mediator, he must involve all groups—employers, news media, unions, financial institutions, and others—which only together can bridge the chasm now separating the racial ghetto from the community. His goal, in effect, must be to develop a new working concept of democracy within the city.

In this effort, state government has a vital role to play. It must provide a fuller measure of financial and other resources to urban areas. The crisis confronting city government today cannot be met without regional cooperation. This cooperation can take many forms—metropolitan government, regional planning, and joint endeavors. But it must be the principal goal, and perhaps the overriding concern, of leadership at the state level to fashion a lasting and mutually productive relationship between city and suburban areas.

We have cited deep hostility between police and ghetto communities as a primary cause of the disorders surveyed by the Commission. In Newark, Detroit, Watts, and Harlem—in practically every city that has experienced racial disruption

It is the mayor's job to create a sense of concern for all of a city's residents. New York Mayor John Lindsay talks with young residents of Harlem.

since the summer of 1964, abrasive relationships between police and Negroes and other minority groups have been a major source of grievance, tension, and ultimately, disorder.

In a fundamental sense, however, it is wrong to define the problem solely as hostility to police. In many ways, the policeman only symbolizes much deeper problems.

The policeman in the ghetto is a symbol not only of law but of the entire system of law enforcement and criminal justice.

As such, he becomes the tangible target for grievances against shortcomings throughout that system: against assembly-line justice in teeming lower courts; against wide disparities in sentences; against antiquated correctional facilities; against the basic inequities imposed by the system on the poor—to whom, for example, the option of bail means only jail.

The policeman in the ghetto is a symbol of increasingly bitter social debate over law enforcement.

One side, disturbed and perplexed by sharp rises in crime and urban violence, exerts extreme pressure on police for tougher law enforcement. Another group, inflamed against police as agents of repression, tends toward defiance of what it regards as order maintained at the expense of justice.

The policeman in the ghetto is the most visible symbol, finally, of a society from which many ghetto Negroes are increasingly alienated.

At the same time, police responsibilities in the ghetto are even greater than elsewhere in the community, since the other institutions of social control have so little authority there. This is true of the schools, because so many are segregated, old, and inferior; of religion, which has become irrelevant to those who have lost faith as they lost hope; of career aspirations, which for many young Negroes are totally lacking; and of the family, because its bonds are so often snapped. It is the policeman who must deal with the consequences of this institutional vacuum, and who is then resented for his presence and for the measures this effort demands.

Alone, the policeman in the ghetto cannot solve these problems. His role is already one of the most difficult in our society. He must deal daily with a range of problems and people that test his patience, ingenuity, character, and courage in ways in which few of us are ever tested. Without positive leadership, goals, operational guidance, and public support, the individual policeman can only feel victimized. Nor are these problems the responsibility only of police adminstrators; they are deep enough to tax the courage, intelligence, and leadership of mayors, city officials, and community leaders. As Dr. Kenneth B. Clark told the Commission:

> This society knows . . . that if human beings are confined in ghetto compounds of our cities, and are subjected to criminally inferior education and pervasive economic and job discrimination, committed to houses unfit for human habitation, subjected to unspeakable conditions of municipal services, such as sanitation, that such human beings are not likely to be responsive to appeals to be lawful, to be respectful, to be concerned with property of others.

To a people imbued with a deep sense of injustice the police have come to symbolize a repressive force barring any hope of escape from the ills that beset them. And while society must aid police in taking every possible step to allay ghetto grievances, it is the police who must bear a major responsibility for making needed changes.

In the first instance, they have the prime responsibility for safeguarding the minimum goal of any civilized society:

*The police must gain the support of the ghetto community.
A policeman makes friends with neighborhood children.*

security of life and property. To do so, they are given society's maximum power: discretion in the use of force.

Second, it is axiomatic that effective law enforcement requires the support of the community. Such support will not be present when a substantial segment of the community feels threatened by the police and regards the police as an occupying force.

At the same time, public officials also have a clear duty to help the police make any necessary changes to minimize as far as possible the risk of further disorders.

To meet the needs arising from five basic problem areas, the Commission recommends that city government and police authorities:

Review police operations in the ghetto to ensure the proper conduct of police officers and eliminate abrasive practices.

Provide more adequate police protection to ghetto residents so as to eliminate their high sense of insecurity and their belief in the existence of a dual standard of law enforcement.

Establish fair and effective mechanisms for the redress of grievances against the police and other municipal employees.

Develop and adopt policy guidelines to assist officers in making critical decisions in areas where police conduct can create tension.

Attempt to insure widespread community support for law enforcement by:

(1) Developing and putting into practice innovative police-community relations programs.

(2) Recruiting more Negroes into the regular police force, and reviewing promotion policies to insure fair promotion for Negro officers.

(3) Establishing a community service officer program to attract ghetto youths between the ages of seventeen and twenty-one to police work. These junior officers would perform duties in ghetto neighborhoods but would not have full police authority. The Fed-

eral government should provide support equal to 90 per cent of the costs of employing community service officers on the basis of one for every ten regular officers.

Community Response to Disorder

To analyze the complex social causes of disorder, to plumb the impact of generations of deprivation, to work for broad and sensitive efforts at prevention are vital tasks. But they are slow and difficult. When, in the meantime, civil disorder breaks out, three simple principles emerge.

First: Preserving civil peace is the first responsibility of government.

Individuals cannot be permitted to endanger the public peace and safety, and public officials have a duty to make it clear that all just and necessary means to protect both will be used. Our society is founded on the rule of law. That rule must prevail; without it, we will lack not only order but the environment essential to social and economic progress.

Second: In maintaining the rule of law, we must be careful not to sacrifice it in the name of order.

In our concern over civil disorder we must not mistake

lawful protest for illegal activities. The guardians of the law are also subject to the laws they serve. As the Federal Bureau of Investigation states in its riot manual for law enforcement officers:

> A peaceful or lawful demonstration should not be looked upon with disapproval by a police agency; rather, it should be considered as a safety valve possibly serving to prevent a riot. The police agency should not countenance violations of law. However, a police agency does not have the right to deny the demonstrator his Constitutional rights.

Third: Maintaining civil order is the responsibility of the entire community.

Not even the most professional and devoted law-enforcement agency alone can quell civil disorder any more than it alone can prevent civil disorder. A thin blue line is too thin. Maintaining civil peace is the responsibility of the entire community, particularly public officials. The guidance, assistance, and support of the mayor can be decisive.

To maintain control of incidents which could lead to disorders, the Commission recommends that local officials:

Assign seasoned, well-trained policemen and supervisory officers to patrol ghetto areas, and to respond to disturbances.

Develop plans which will quickly muster maximum police manpower and highly qualified senior commanders at the outbreak of disorders.

Provide special training in the prevention of disorders, and prepare police for riot control and for operation in units with adequate command and control and field communication for proper discipline and effectiveness.

Develop guidelines governing the use of control equipment and provide alternatives to the use of lethal weapons. Federal support for research in this area is needed.

Establish an intelligence system to provide police and other public officials with reliable information that may help to prevent the outbreak of a disorder and to institute effective control measures in the event that a riot erupts.

Develop continuing contacts with ghetto residents to make use of the forces for order which exist within the community.

Establish machinery for neutralizing rumors and enabling Negro leaders and residents to obtain the facts. Create special rumor details to collect, evaluate, and dispel rumors that may lead to a civil disorder.

The Commission believes there is a grave danger that some law-enforcement agencies may resort to the indiscriminate and excessive use of force. The harmful effects of overreaction are incalculable. The Commission condemns moves to equip police departments with mass-destruction weapons, such as automatic rifles, machine guns, and tanks. Weapons which are designed to destroy, not to control, have no place in densely populated urban communities.

The Commission recommends that the Federal government share in the financing of programs for improvement of police forces, both in their normal law-enforcement activities and in their response to civil disorders.

A riot in the city poses a separate crisis in the administration of justice. Partially paralyzed by decades of neglect, deficient in facilities, procedures, and personnel, and overwhelmed by the demands of normal operations, lower courts have staggered under the crushing new burdens of civil disorders.

Some of our courts, moreover, have lost the confidence of the poor. This judgment is underwritten by the members and staff of this Commission, who have gone into the courthouses and ghettos of the cities torn by the riots of 1967.

The belief is pervasive among ghetto residents that lower courts in our urban communities dispense "assembly-line" justice; that from arrest to sentencing, the poor and uneducated are denied equal justice with the affluent; that procedures such as bail and fines have been perverted to perpetuate class inequities. We have found that the apparatus of justice in some areas has itself become a focus for distrust and hostility. Too often the courts have operated to aggravate rather than relieve the tensions that ignite and fire disorders.

The quality of justice which the courts dispense in time of civil crisis is one of the indices of the capacity of a democratic society to survive. To see that this quality does not become strained is therefore a task of critical importance.

"No program of crime prevention," the President's Commission on Law Enforcement and the Administration of Justice found, "will be effective without a massive overhaul of the lower criminal courts." The range of needed reforms recommended in their report is broad, calling for:

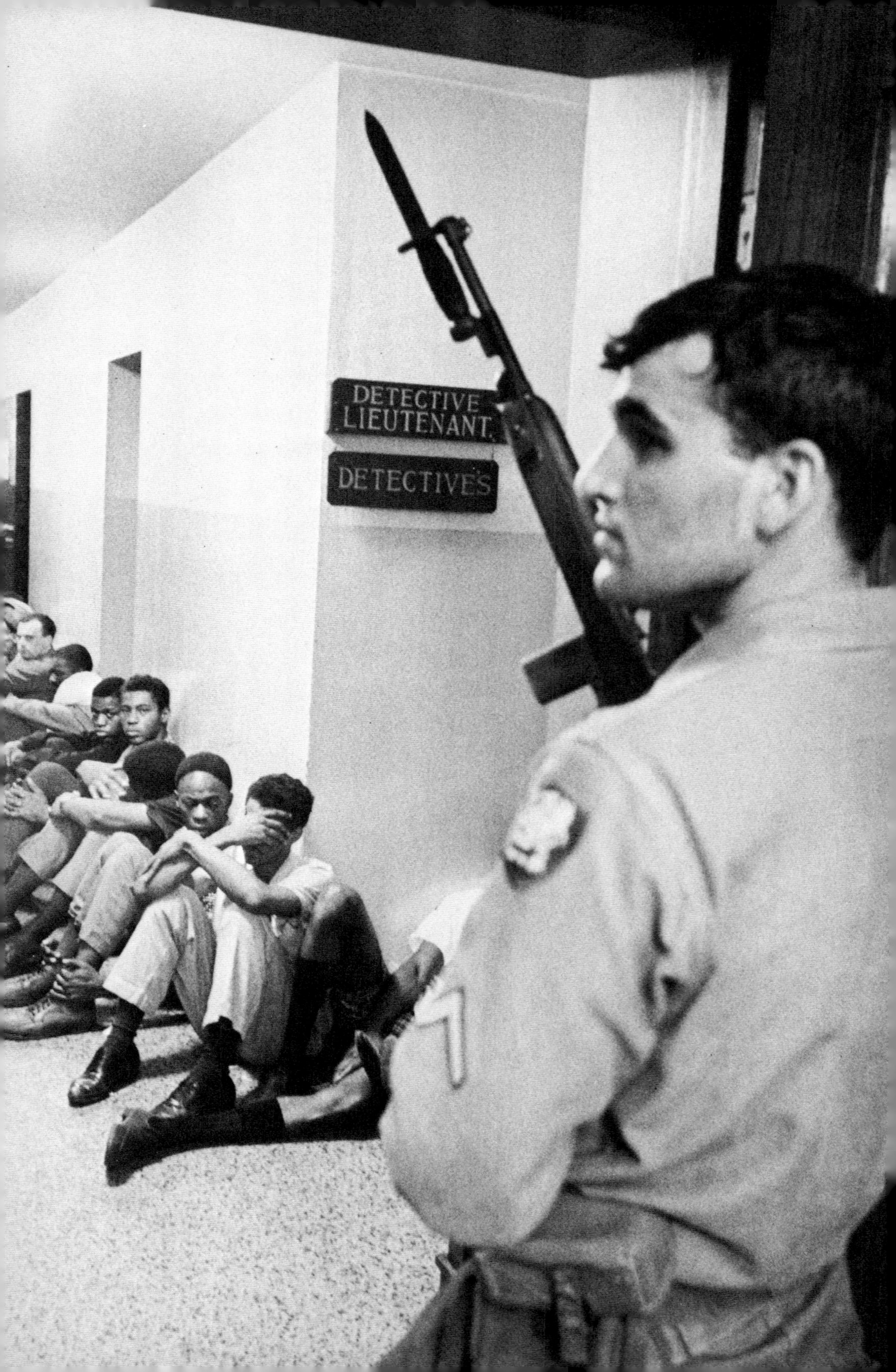
DETECTIVE
LIEUTENANT.
DETECTIVES

Increasing judicial manpower and reforming the selection and tenure of judges.

Providing more prosecutors, defense counsel, and probation officers, and training them adequately.

Modernizing the physical facilities and administration of the courts.

Creating unified state court systems.

Coordinating state-wide the operations of local prosecutors.

Improving the informational bases for pretrial screening and negotiated pleas.

Revising the bail system and setting up systems for stationhouse summons and release for persons accused of certain offenses.

Revising sentencing laws and policies toward a more just structure.

If we are to provide our judicial institutions with sufficient capacity to cope effectively with civil disorders, those reforms are vitally necessary. They are long overdue. The responsibility for this effort will rest heavily on the organized bar of the community. The prevalence of "assembly-line" justice is evidence that in many localities the bar has not met its leadership responsibilities.

The Commission recommends that the cities and states:

Undertake reform of the lower courts so as to improve the quality of justice rendered under normal conditions.

Plan comprehensive measures by which the criminal justice system may be supplemented during civil disorders so that its deliberative functions are protected and the quality of justice is maintained.

Such emergency plans require broad community participation and dedicated leadership by the bench and bar. Emergency plans should include:

Laws sufficient to deter and punish riot conduct.

Suspects waiting to be booked during the Detroit riot

Additional judges, bail, and probation officers, and clerical staff.

Arrangements for volunteer lawyers to help prosecutors and to represent riot defendants at every stage of proceedings.

Policies to insure proper and individual bail, arraignment, pretrial, trial, and sentencing proceedings.

Adequate emergency processing and detention facilities.

The President, in his charge to the Commission, requested advice on the "proper public role in helping cities repair the damage" suffered in the recent disorders.

Damage took many forms. In Detroit alone, forty-three persons were killed, many of whom were heads of families. Over six hundred persons were injured. Fire destroyed or badly damaged at least a hundred single and two-family dwellings. Stores of all kinds were looted and burned. Hundreds of businesses lost revenue by complying with a curfew, and thousands of citizens lost wages because businesses were closed. As the riot came to an end, streets and sidewalks were strewn with rubble, and citizens were imperiled by the shells of burned-out buildings verging on collapse.

In 1965 Watts suffered a similar pattern of damage and injury. Injury was also widespread in Newark. In most other disorders the extent of the damage was far less, but in almost all a few persons suffered severe physical or financial injury.

Some losses, such as pain and suffering, cannot be repaired or compensated. Others are normally handled through private insurance. The Commission believes that legislation should be enacted to provide fuller assistance to communities and to help expand the private insurance mechanism for compensating individuals for their losses.

The Commission recommends that the Federal government:

Amend the Federal Disaster Act—which now applies only to natural disasters—to permit the Federal government to provide emergency food and medical assistance to cities during major civil disorders, and long-term economic assistance afterward.

With the cooperation of the states, create incentives for the private insurance industry to provide more adequate property-insurance coverage in inner-city areas.

In his charge to the Commission, the President asked: "What effect do the mass media have on the riots?"

The Commission determined that the answer to the President's question did not lie solely in the performance of the press and broadcasters in reporting the riots. Our analysis had to consider also the overall treatment by the media of the Negro ghettos, community relations, racial attitudes, and poverty—day by day and month by month, year in and year out.

A wide range of interviews with government officials, law-enforcement authorities, media personnel, and other citizens, including ghetto residents, as well as a quantitative analysis of riot coverage and a special conference with industry representatives, leads us to conclude that:

Despite instances of sensationalism, inaccuracy, and distortion, newspapers, radio, and television tried on the whole to give a balanced, factual account of the 1967 disorders.

Elements of the news media failed to portray accurately the scale and character of the violence that occurred last summer. The overall effect was, we believe, an exaggeration of both mood and event.

Most important, the media failed to report adequately on the causes and consequences of civil disorders and on the underlying problems of race relations. They have not communicated to the majority of their audience—which is white—a sense of the degradation, misery, and hopelessness of life in the ghetto. They have not shown understanding or appreciation of—and thus have not communicated—a sense of Negro culture and history.

These failings must be corrected, and the improvement must come from within the industry. Freedom of the press is not the issue. Any effort to impose governmental restrictions would be inconsistent with fundamental Constitutional precepts.

We have seen evidence that the news media are becoming aware of and concerned about their performance in this field. As that concern grows, coverage will improve. But much more must be done, and it must be done soon.

The Commission recommends that the media:

Expand coverage of the Negro community and of race problems through the permanent assignment of reporters familiar with urban and racial affairs, and through the establishment of more and better links with the Negro community.

Integrate Negroes and Negro activities into all aspects of coverage and content, including newspaper articles and television programing, so that the Negro is portrayed as a matter of routine and in the context of the total society. The news media must publish newspapers and produce programs that recognize the existence and activities of Negroes, both as Negroes and as part of the larger community.

Recruit more Negroes into journalism and broadcasting and promote those who are qualified to positions of significant responsibility. Recruitment should begin in high schools and continue through college; where necessary, aid for training should be provided.

Improve coordination with police in reporting riot news through advance planning, and cooperate with the police in the designation of police information officers, establishment of information centers, and development of mutually acceptable guidelines for riot reporting and the conduct of media personnel.

Accelerate efforts to insure accurate and responsible reporting of riot and racial news, through the adoption by all news-gathering organizations of stringent internal staff guidelines.

Cooperate in the establishment of a privately organized and funded Institute of Urban Communications to train and educate journalists in urban affairs, recruit and train more Negro journalists, develop methods for improving police-press relations, review coverage of riots and racial issues, and support continuing research in the urban field.

The Future of the Cities

We believe action of the kind outlined in preceding pages can contribute substantially to control of disorders in the near future. But there should be no mistake about the long run. The underlying forces continue to gain momentum.

The most basic of these is the accelerating segregation of low-income, disadvantaged Negroes within the ghettos of the largest American cities.

By 1985 the Negro population in central cities is expected to increase by 68 per cent to approximately 20.3 million. Coupled with the continued exodus of white families to the suburbs, this growth will produce majority Negro populations in many of the nation's largest cities.

The future of these cities, and of their burgeoning Negro populations, is grim. Most new employment opportunities are being created in suburbs and outlying areas. This trend will continue unless important changes in public policy are made.

The prospect, therefore, is further deterioration of already inadequate municipal tax bases in the face of increasing demands for public services, and continuing unemployment and poverty among the urban Negro population.

Three choices are open to the nation:

We can maintain present policies. This would mean continuing to spend the proportion of the nation's resources now allocated to programs for the unemployed and the disadvantaged, and persisting in our inadequate and failing effort to achieve an integrated society.

We can adopt a policy of "enrichment," aimed at improving dramatically the quality of ghetto life while abandoning integration as a goal.

We can pursue integration by combining ghetto "enrichment" with policies which will encourage Negro movement out of central city areas.

Under the present policies choice, the nation would maintain approximately the share of resources now being allocated to programs of assistance for the poor, unemployed, and disadvantaged. These programs are likely to grow (given continuing economic growth and rising Federal revenues), but they will not grow fast enough to stop, let alone reverse, the already deteriorating quality of life in central-city ghettos.

This choice carries the highest ultimate price, as we will point out.

Under the enrichment choice, the nation would seek to offset the effects of continued Negro segregation and deprivation in large city ghettos. The enrichment choice would aim at creating dramatic improvements in the quality of life in disadvantaged central-city neighborhoods—both white and Negro. It would require marked increases in Federal spending for education, housing, employment, job training, and social services.

The enrichment choice would seek to lift poor Negroes and whites above poverty status and thereby give them the capacity to enter the mainstream of American life. But it would not, at least for many years, appreciably affect either the increasing concentration of Negroes in the ghetto or racial segregation in residential areas outside the ghetto.

The integration choice would be aimed at reversing the movement of the country toward two societies, separate and unequal. It—like the enrichment choice—would call for large-scale improvement in the quality of ghetto life. But it would also involve both creating strong incentives for Negro movement out of central-city ghettos and enlarging freedom of choice concerning housing, employment, and schools.

The result would fall considerably short of full integration. The experience of other ethnic groups indicates that some Negro households would be scattered in largely white residential areas. Others—probably in larger number—would voluntarily cluster together in largely Negro neighborhoods. The integration choice would thus produce both integration and segregation. But the segregation would be voluntary.

Articulating these three choices plainly oversimplifies the possibilities open to the country. We believe, however, that they encompass the basic issues—issues which the American public must face if it is serious in its concern not only about civil disorder but about the future of our democratic society.

The Present Policies Choice Powerful forces of social and political inertia are moving the country steadily along the course of existing policies toward a divided country. This course may well involve changes in many social and economic programs—but not enough to produce fundamental alterations in the key factors of Negro concentration, racial segregation, and the lack of sufficient enrichment to arrest the decay of deprived neighborhoods.

Some movement toward enrichment can be found in efforts to encourage industries to locate plants in central cities, in increased Federal expenditures for education, in the important concepts embodied in the War on Poverty, and in the Model Cities Program. But Congressional appropriations for even present Federal programs have been so small that they fall short of effective enrichment.

As for challenging concentration and segregation, a national commitment to this purpose has yet to develop.

Of the three future courses we have defined, the present policies choice—the choice we are now making—is the course with the most ominous consequences for our democratic society. We believe that the present policies choice would lead to a larger number of violent incidents of the kind that have stimulated recent major disorders.

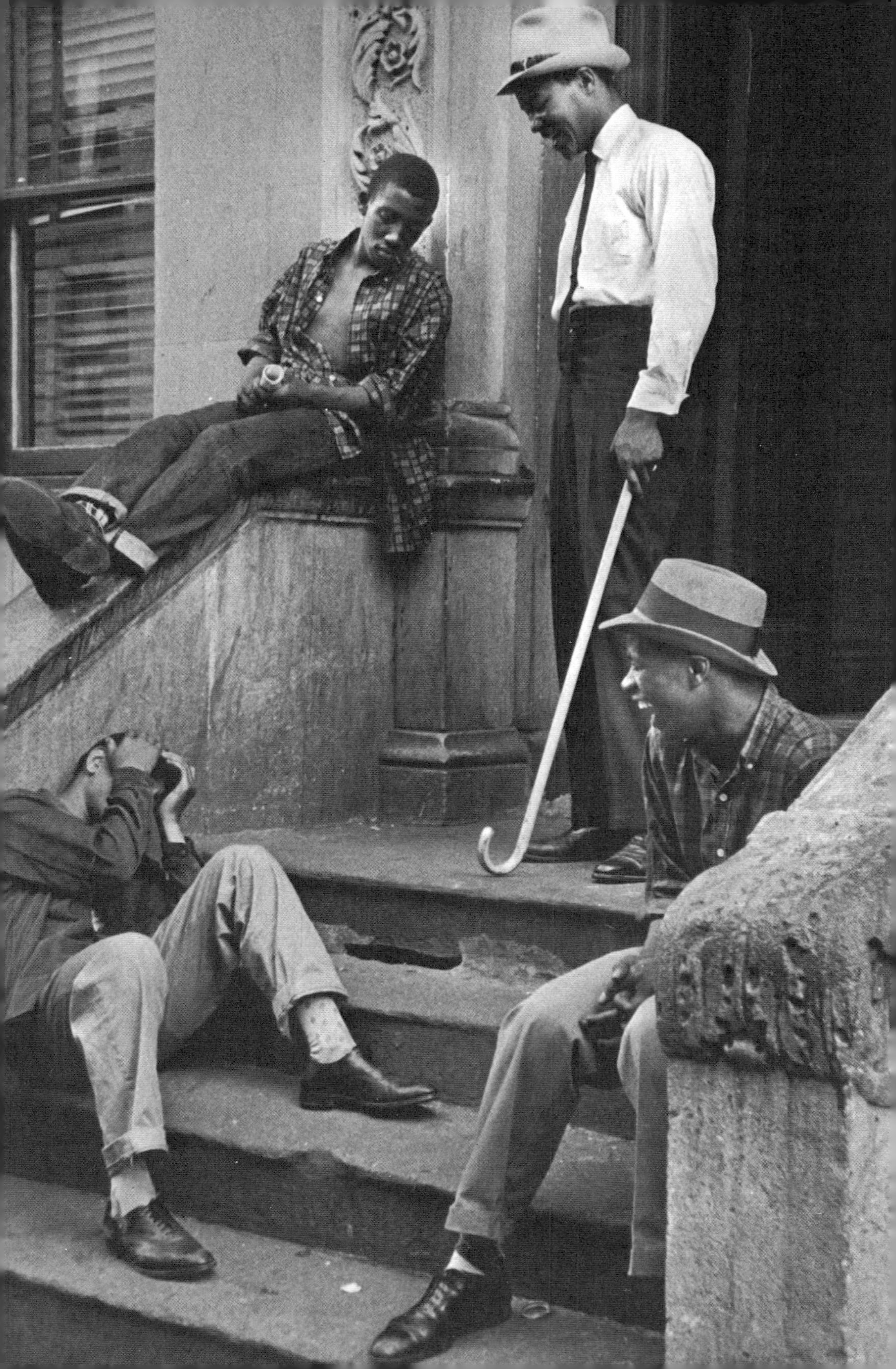

First, it does nothing to raise the hopes, absorb the energies, or constructively challenge the talents of the rapidly growing number of young Negro men in central cities. The proportion of unemployed or underemployed among them will remain very high. These young men have contributed disproportionately to crime and violence in cities in the past, and there is danger, obviously, that they will continue to do so.

Second, under these conditions a rising proportion of Negroes in disadvantaged city areas might come to look upon the deprivation and segregation they suffer as proper justification for violent protest or for extending support to now isolated extremists who advocate civil disruption by guerrilla tactics.

More incidents would not necessarily mean more or worse riots. For the near future there is a substantial likelihood that even an increased number of incidents could be controlled before becoming major disorders—if society undertakes to improve police and National Guard forces so that they can respond to potential disorders with more prompt and disciplined use of force.

In fact, the likelihood of incidents mushrooming into major disorders would be only slightly higher in the near future under the present policies choice than under the other two possible choices. For no new policies or programs could possibly alter basic ghetto conditions immediately. And the announcement of new programs under the other choices would generate new expectations. Expectations inevitably outrun performance. In the short run they might even increase the level of frustration.

In the long run, however, the present policies choice risks a seriously greater probability of major disorders, worse, possibly, than those already experienced.

224 WHAT CAN BE DONE?

If the Negro population as a whole developed even stronger feelings of being wrongly "penned in" and discriminated against, many of its members might come to support not only riots but the rebellion now being preached by only a handful. If large-scale violence resulted, white retaliation would follow. This spiral could quite conceivably lead to a kind of urban *apartheid* with semimartial law in many major cities, enforced residence of Negroes in segregated areas, and a drastic reduction in personal freedom for all Americans, particularly Negroes.

The same distinction is applicable to the cost of the present policies choice. In the short run, its costs—at least its direct cash outlays—would be far less than for other choices.

Social and economic programs likely to have significant, lasting effect would require very substantial annual appropriations for many years. Their cost would far exceed the direct losses sustained in recent civil disorders. Property damage in all the disorders we investigated, including Detroit and Newark, totaled less than 100 million dollars.

But it would be a tragic mistake to view the present policies as cheap. Damage figures measure only a small part of the cost of civil disorder. They cannot measure the costs in terms of the lives lost, injuries suffered, minds and attitudes closed and frozen in prejudice, or the hidden costs of the profound disruption of entire cities.

Ultimately, moreover, the economic and social costs of the present policies choice would far surpass the cost of the alternatives. The rising concentration of impoverished Negroes and other minorities within the urban ghettos will constantly expand public expenditures for welfare, law enforcement, and unemployment and other existing programs without arresting the decay of older city neighborhoods and the breeding of frustration and discontent.

But the most significant item on the balance of accounts will remain largely invisible and incalculable—the toll in human values taken by continued poverty, segregation, and inequality of opportunity.

Another and equally serious consequence of the present policies choice is the fact that this course would lead to the permanent establishment of two societies: one predominantly white and located in the suburbs, in smaller cities, and in outlying areas, and one largely Negro, located in central cities.

We are well on the way to just such a divided nation.

This division is veiled by the fact that Negroes do not now dominate many central cities. But they soon will, as we have shown, and the new Negro mayors will be facing even more difficult conditions than now exist.

As Negroes succeed whites in our largest cities, the proportion of low-income residents in those cities will probably increase. This is likely even if both white and Negro incomes continue to rise at recent rates, because Negroes have much lower incomes than whites. Moreover, many of the ills of large central cities spring from their age, their location, and the obsolescence of their physical structures. The deterioration and economic decay stemming from these factors have been proceeding for decades and will continue to plague older cities regardless of who resides in them.

These facts underlie the fourfold dilemma of the American city:

Fewer tax dollars come in as large numbers of middle-income taxpayers move out of central cities and property values and business decline.

More tax dollars are required to provide essential public services and facilities and to meet the needs of expanding lower-income groups.

Each tax dollar buys less, because of increasing costs.

Citizen dissatisfaction with municipal services grows as needs, expectations, and standards of living increase throughout the community.

These are the conditions which would greet the Negro-dominated municipal governments that will gradually come to power in many of our major cities. The Negro electorates in those cities probably would demand basic changes in present policies. Like the present white electorates there, they would have to look to two basic sources for assistance: the private sector and the Federal government.

With respect to the private sector, major private capital investment in those cities might have ceased almost altogether if white-dominated firms and industries had decided the risks and costs were too great. The withdrawal of private capital is already far advanced in most all-Negro areas of our large cities.

Even if private investment continued, it alone would not suffice. Big cities containing high proportions of low-income Negroes and block after block of deteriorating older property need very substantial assistance from the Federal government to meet the demands of their electorates for improved services and living conditions.

It is probable, however, that Congress will be the most heavily influenced by representatives of the suburban and outlying city electorate. These areas will comprise 40 per cent of our total population by 1985, as compared with 31 per cent in 1960; and central cities will decline from 32 per cent to 27 per cent (figures based on Census Bureau series D projections).

Since even the suburbs will be feeling the squeeze of higher local government costs, Congress might resist providing the extensive assistance which central cities will desperately need.

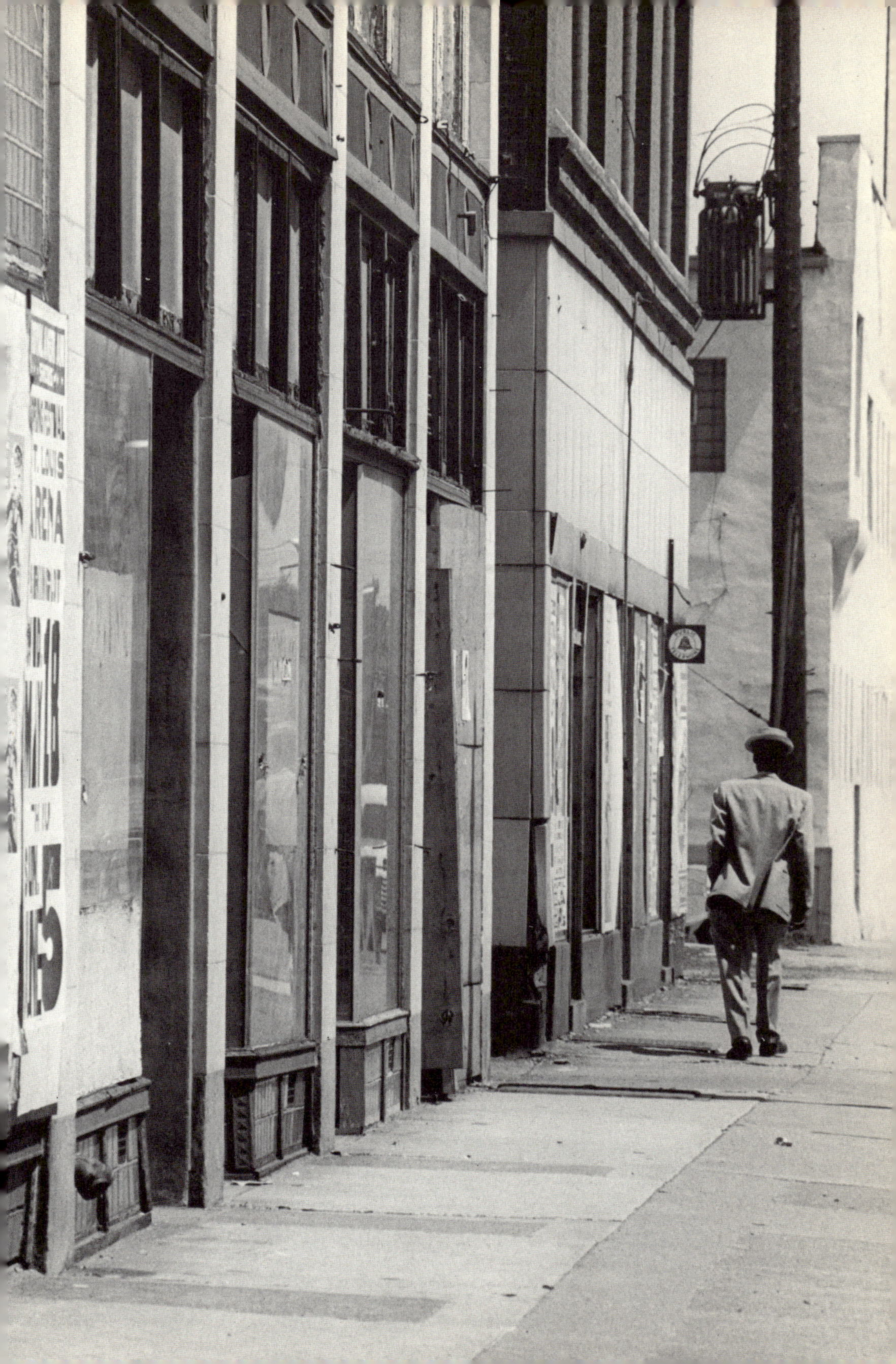
T. LOUIS
ARENA

Thus the present policies choice, if pursued for any length of time, might force simultaneous political and economic polarization in many of our largest metropolitan areas. Such polarization would involve, on the one hand, large central cities—mainly Negro, with many poor, and nearly bankrupt; and on the other hand, most of our suburbs—mainly white, generally affluent, but heavily taxed.

Some areas might avoid political confrontation by shifting to some form of metropolitan government designed to offer regional solutions for such pressing urban problems as property taxation, air and water pollution, refuse disposal, and commuter transport. Yet this would hardly eliminate the basic segregation and relative poverty of the urban Negro population. It might even increase the Negro's sense of frustration and alienation if it operated to prevent Negro political control of central cities.

The acquisition of power by Negro-dominated governments in central cities is surely a legitimate and desirable exercise of political power by a minority group. It is in an American political tradition exemplified by the achievements of the Irish in New York and Boston.

But such Negro political development would also involve virtually complete racial segregation and virtually complete spatial separation. By 1985 the separate Negro society in our central cities would contain almost 21 million citizens. That is almost 68 per cent larger than the present Negro population of central cities. It is also larger than the current population of every Negro nation in Africa except Nigeria.

If developing a racially integrated society is extraordinarily difficult today when 12.1 million Negroes live in central cities, then it is quite clearly going to be virtually impossible in 1985 when almost 21 million Negroes—still much poorer and less educated than most whites—will be living there.

There are at least two possible developments under the present policies choice which might avert such polarization. The first is a faster increase in incomes among Negroes than has occurred in the recent past. This might prevent central cities from becoming even deeper "poverty traps" than they now are. This fact suggests the importance of effective job programs and higher levels of welfare payments for dependent families.

The second possible development is migration of a growing Negro middle class out of the central city. This would not prevent competition for Federal funds between central cities and outlying areas, but it might diminish the racial undertones of that competition.

There is, however, no evidence that a continuation of present policies would be accompanied by any such movement. There is already a significant Negro middle class. It grew rapidly from 1960 to 1966. Yet in these years 88.9 per cent of the total national growth of Negro population was concentrated in central cities—the highest in history. Indeed, from 1960 to 1966 there was actually a net total migration of Negroes from the urban fringes of metropolitan areas into central cities. The Commission believes it unlikely that this trend will suddenly reverse itself without significant changes in private attitudes and public policies.

The Enrichment Choice The present policies choice plainly would involve the continuation of efforts such as the Model Cities Program, manpower programs, and the War on Poverty. These are in fact enrichment programs, designed to improve the quality of life in the ghetto.

Because of their limited scope and funds, however, they constitute only very modest steps toward enrichment—and would continue to do so even if these programs were somewhat enlarged or supplemented.

The premise of the enrichment choice is performance. To adopt this choice would require a substantially greater share of national resources—sufficient to make a dramatic, visible impact on life in the urban Negro ghetto.

Effective enrichment policies probably would have three immediate effects on civil disorders.

First, the announcement of specific large-scale programs and the demonstration of a strong intent to carry them out might persuade ghetto residents that genuine remedies for their problems were forthcoming, thereby allaying tensions.

Second, such announcements would strongly stimulate the aspirations and hopes of members of these communities—possibly well beyond the capabilities of society to deliver and to do so promptly. This might increase frustration and discontent, to some extent canceling the first effect.

Third, if there could be immediate action on meaningful job training and the creation of productive jobs for large numbers of unemployed young people, they would become much less likely to engage in civil disorders.

Such action is difficult now, when there are about 585,000 young Negro men aged fourteen to twenty-four in central cities—of whom 81,000, or 13.8 per cent, are unemployed, and probably two or three times as many are underemployed. It will not become easier in the future. By 1975 this age group will have grown to approximately 700,000.

Given the size of the present problem, plus the large growth of this age group, the creation of sufficient meaningful jobs will require extensive programs, begun rapidly. Even if the nation is willing to embark on such programs, there is no certainty that they can be made effective soon enough.

Consequently, there is no certainty that the enrichment

Jobs for young men are provided by a project to build a vest-pocket park in Harlem (top), and in Job Corps training for construction work.

choice would do much more in the near future to diminish violent incidents in central cities than would the present policies choice. However, if enrichment programs can succeed in meeting the needs of residents of disadvantaged areas for jobs, education, housing, and city services, then over the years this choice is almost certain to reduce both the level and frequency of urban disorder.

One objective of the enrichment choice would be to help as many disadvantaged Americans as possible—of all races—to enter the mainstream of American prosperity, to progress toward what is often called middle-class status. If the enrichment choice were adopted, it could certainly attain this objective to a far greater degree than would the present policies choice. This could significantly change the quality of life in many central-city areas.

It can be argued that a rapidly enlarging Negro middle class would also promote Negro migration out of the central cities, and that the enrichment choice would thus open up an escape hatch from the ghetto. This argument, however, has two weaknesses.

The first is experience. Central cities already have sizable and growing numbers of middle-class Negro families. Yet only a few have migrated from the central city. The past pattern of gradual movement from central-city areas to middle-class suburbs characteristic of white ethnic groups has not applied to Negroes. Effective open-housing laws will help make this possible, but it is probable that other more extensive changes in policies and attitudes will be required—and these would extend beyond the enrichment choice.

The second weakness in the argument is time. Even if enlargement of the Negro middle class succeeded in encouraging movement out of the central city, it could not do so fast enough to offset the rapid growth of the ghetto.

To offset even *half* the estimated growth of the ghetto by 1975, a migration from central cities of 217,000 persons a year would be required. This is eight times the annual increase in suburban Negro population—including natural increase—that occurred from 1960 to 1966. Even the most effective enrichment program is not likely to accomplish this.

A corollary problem derives from the continuing migration of poor Negroes from Southern to Northern and Western cities. Adoption of the enrichment choice would require large-scale efforts to improve conditions in the South sufficiently to remove the pressure to migrate. Under present conditions, slightly over a third of the estimated increase in Negro central-city population by 1985 will result from migration—3.0 million out of a total increase of 8.2 million.

The enrichment choice is in line with some of the currents of Negro protest thought that fall under the label of "Black Power." We do not refer to versions of Black Power ideology which promote violence, generate racial hatred, or advocate total separation of the races. Rather, we mean the view which asserts that the American Negro population can assume its proper role in society and overcome its feelings of powerlessness and lack of self-respect only by gaining the power to make the decisions which directly affect its own members. A fully integrated society is not thought possible until the Negro minority within the ghetto has developed political strength—a strong bargaining position from which to deal with the rest of society.

In short, this argument would regard predominantly Negro central cities and predominantly white outlying areas, not as harmful, but as an advantageous future.

Proponents of these views also focus on the need for the Negro to organize economically as well as politically, thus tapping new energies and resources for self-development.

One of the hardest tasks in improving disadvantaged areas is to discover how deeply-deprived residents can develop their own capabilities by participating more fully in decisions and activities which affect them. Such learning-by-doing efforts are a vital part of the process of bringing deprived people into the social mainstream.

The enrichment choice by no means seeks to perpetuate racial segregation. In the end, however, its premise is that disadvantaged Negroes can achieve equality of opportunity with whites while continuing in conditions of nearly complete separation.

This premise has been vigorously advocated by Black Power proponents. While most Negroes originally desired racial integration, many are losing hope of ever achieving it because of seemingly implacable white resistance. Yet they cannot bring themselves to accept the conclusion that most of the millions of Negroes who are forced to live racially segregated lives must therefore be condemned to inferior lives—to inferior education, or inferior housing, or inferior status.

Rather, they reason, there must be some way to make the quality of life in the ghetto areas just as good—or better—than elsewhere. It is not surprising that some Black Power advocates are denouncing integration and claiming that, given the hypocrisy and racism that pervade white society, life in a black society is, in fact, morally superior. This argument is understandable, but there is a great deal of evidence that it is unrealistic.

The economy of the United States and particularly the sources of employment are preponderantly white. In this circumstance, a policy of separate but equal employment could only relegate Negroes permanently to inferior incomes and economic status.

The best evidence regarding education is contained in recent reports of the Office of Education and Civil Rights Commission, which suggest that both racial and economic integration are essential to educational equality for Negroes. Yet critics point out that, certainly until integration is achieved, various types of enrichment programs must be tested, and that dramatic changes may result from intensive educational enrichment—such as far smaller classes, or greatly expanded preschool programs, or changes in the home environment of Negro children resulting from steady jobs for fathers.

Still others advocate shifting control over ghetto schools from professional administrators to local residents. This, they say, would improve curricula, give students a greater sense of their own value, and thus raise their morale and educational achievement. These approaches have not yet been tested sufficiently.

One conclusion, however, does seem reasonable: Any real improvement in the quality of education in low-income, all-Negro areas will cost a great deal more money than is now being spent there—and perhaps more than is being spent per pupil anywhere. Racial and social-class integration of schools may produce an equal improvement in achievement at less total cost.

Whether or not enrichment in ghetto areas will really work is not yet known, but the enrichment choice is based on the yet-unproven premise that it will. Certainly, enrichment programs could significantly improve existing ghetto schools if they impelled major innovations. But separate-but-equal ghetto education cannot meet the long-range fundamental educational needs of the central-city Negro population.

The three basic educational choices are: providing Negro children with quality education in integrated schools; pro-

A Headstart class

viding them with quality education by enriching ghetto schools; or continuing to provide many Negro children with inferior education in racially segregated school systems, and thus severely limiting their lifetime opportunities.

Consciously or not, it is the third choice that the nation is now making, and this choice the Commission rejects totally.

In the field of housing, it is obvious that "separate but equal" does not mean really equal. The enrichment choice could greatly improve the quantity, variety, and environment of housing available to the ghetto population. It could not provide Negroes with the same freedom and range of choice as whites with equal incomes have. Smaller cities and suburban areas together with the central city provide a far greater variety of housing and environmental settings than the central city alone. Programs to provide housing outside central cities, however, extend beyond the bounds of the enrichment choice.

In the end, whatever its benefits, the enrichment choice might well invite a prospect similar to that of the present policies choice: separate white and black societies.

If enrichment programs were effective, they could greatly narrow the gap in income, education, housing, jobs, and other qualities of life between the ghetto and the mainstream. Hence the chances of harsh polarization—or of disorder—in the next twenty years would be greatly reduced.

Whether they would be reduced far enough depends upon the scope of the programs. Even if the present gap were narrowed, it still could remain as a strong source of tension. History teaches that men are not necessarily placated even by great absolute progress. The controlling factor is relative progress—whether they still perceive a significant gap between themselves and others whom they regard as no more deserving.

Widespread perception of such a gap—and the consequent resentment—might well characterize the situation twenty years from now if the enrichment choice is adopted, for making this choice is essentially another way of choosing a permanently divided country.

The Integration Choice The third and last course open to the nation combines enrichment with programs designed to encourage integration of substantial numbers of Negroes into the society outside the ghetto.

Enrichment must be an important adjunct to any integration course. No matter how ambitious or energetic such a program may be, relatively few Negroes now living in central-city ghettos would be quickly integrated. In the meantime, significant improvement in their present environment is essential.

The enrichment aspect of this third choice should, however, be recognized as interim action designed to expand and create programs that would improve education and earning power. The length of the interim period surely would vary. For some it might be long. But in any event, what should be clearly recognized is that enrichment is only a means toward the goal; it is not the goal.

The goal must be achieving freedom for every citizen to live and work according to his capacities and desires, not his color.

We believe there are four important reasons why American society must give this course the most serious consideration. First, future jobs are being created primarily in the suburbs, while the chronically unemployed population is increasingly concentrated in the ghetto. This separation will make it more and more difficult for Negroes to achieve any-

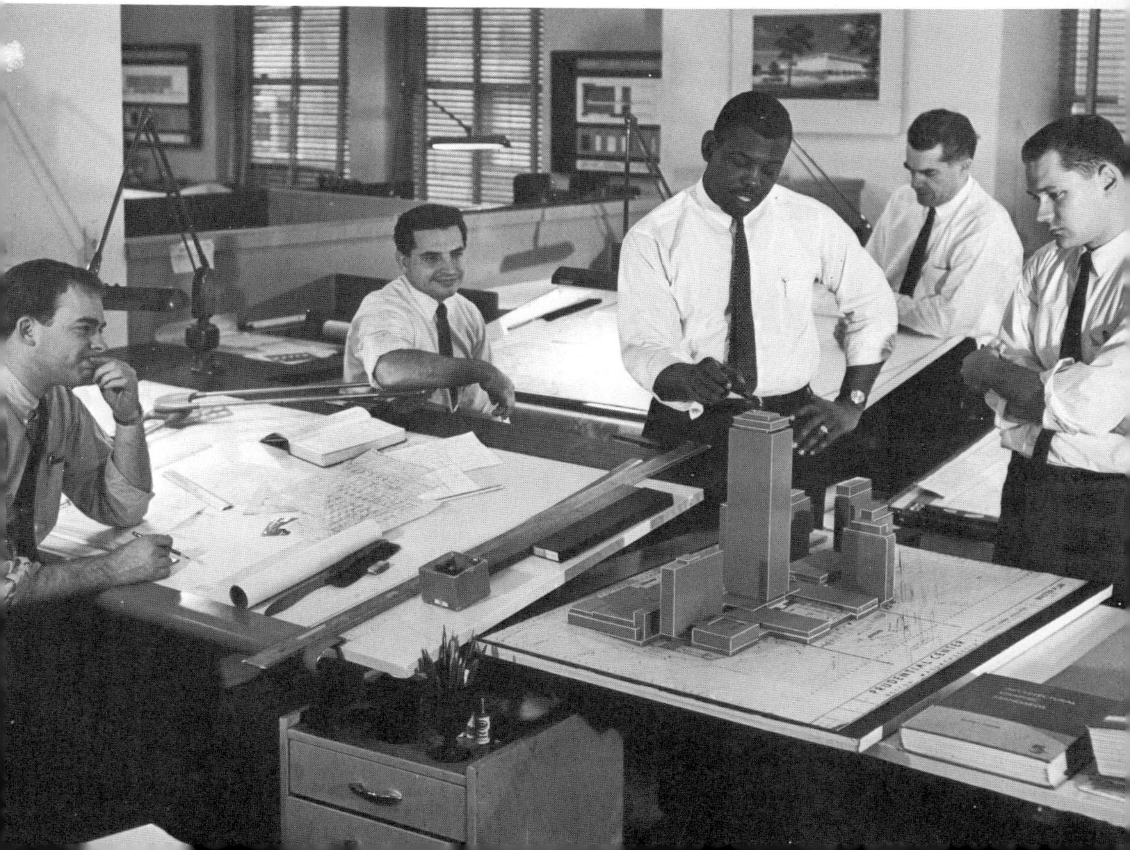
PRUDENTIAL CENTER

thing like full employment in decent jobs. But if, over time, these residents were to begin to find housing outside central cities, they would have access to more knowledge of job opportunities, much shorter trips to reach jobs, and a far better chance of securing employment on a self-sustaining basis.

Second, in the judgment of this Commission, racial and social-class integration is the most effective way of improving the education of ghetto children.

Third, developing an adequate housing supply for low-income and middle-income families, and true freedom of choice in housing for Negroes of all income levels, will require substantial movement from the cities to the suburbs. We do not believe that such movement will occur spontaneously merely as a result of increasing prosperity among Negroes in central cities. A national fair-housing law is essential to begin such a movement. In many suburban areas a program combining positive incentives with the building of new housing will be necessary to carry it out.

Fourth, and by far the most important, integration is the only course which explicitly seeks to achieve a single nation rather than accepting the present movement toward a dual society. This choice would enable us at least to begin reversing the profoundly divisive trend already so evident in our metropolitan areas—before it becomes irreversible.

The future of our cities is neither something which will just happen nor something which will be imposed upon us by an inevitable destiny. That future will be shaped to an important degree by choices we make now.

We have attempted to set forth the major choices because we believe it is vital for Americans to understand the consequences of our present drift.

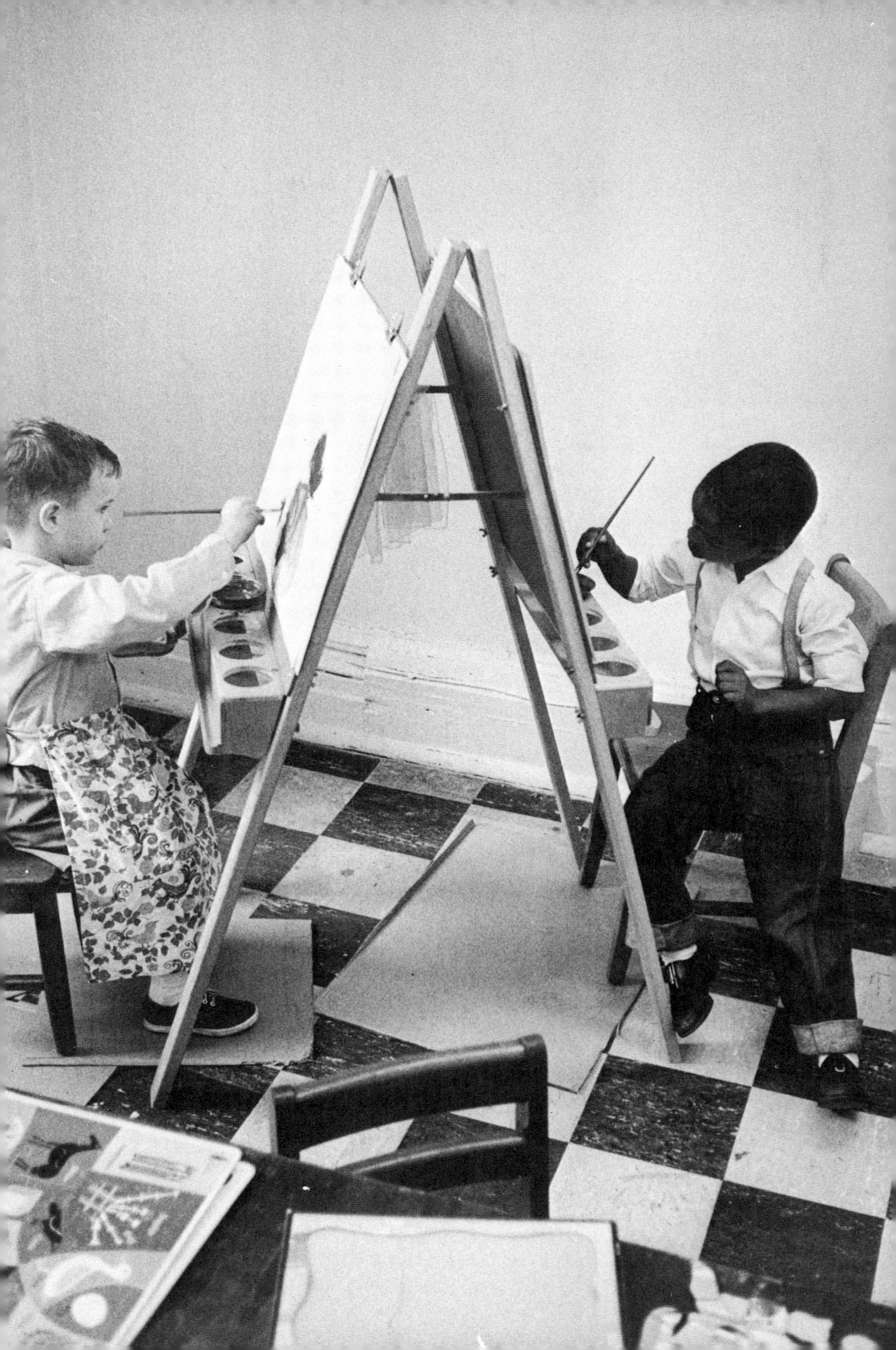

The nation is rapidly moving toward two increasingly separate Americas. Within two decades, this division could be so deep that it would be almost impossible to unite:

(1) A white society principally located in suburbs, in smaller central cities, and in the peripheral parts of large central cities, and

(2) A Negro society largely concentrated within large central cities.

The Negro society will be permanently relegated to its current status, possibly even if we expend great amounts of money and effort in trying to "gild" the ghetto.

In the long run, continuation and expansion of such a permanent division threatens us with two perils.

The first is the danger of sustained violence in our cities. The timing, scale, nature, and repercussions of such violence cannot be foreseen. But if it occurred, it would further destroy our ability to achieve the basic American promises of liberty, justice, and equality.

The second is the danger of a conclusive repudiation of the traditional American ideals of individual dignity, freedom, and equality of opportunity. We will not be able to espouse these ideals in a way that is meaningful to the rest of the world, to ourselves, to our children. Our children may still recite the Pledge of Allegiance and say "one nation indivisible." But they will be learning cynicism, not patriotism.

We cannot escape responsibility for choosing the future of our metropolitan areas and the human relations which develop within them. It is a responsibility so critical that even an unconscious choice to continue present policies has the gravest implications.

The fact that we have delayed in choosing, or by delaying, may be making the wrong choice, does not sentence us either to separatism or to despair. But we must choose. We will choose. Indeed, we are now choosing.

One of the first witnesses to be invited to appear before this Commission was Dr. Kenneth B. Clark, a distinguished and perceptive scholar. Referring to the reports of earlier riot commissions, he said:

> I read that report . . . of the 1919 riot in Chicago, and it is as if I were reading the report of the investigating committee on the Harlem riot of 1935, the report of the investigating committee on the Harlem riot of 1943, the report of the McCone Commission on the Watts riot.
>
> I must again in candor say to you members of this Commission—it is a kind of Alice in Wonderland, with the same moving picture reshown over and over again, the same analysis, the same recommendations, and the same inaction.

These words come to our minds as we conclude this Report.

We have provided an honest beginning. We have learned much. But we have uncovered no startling truths, no unique insights, no simple solutions. The destruction and the bitterness of racial disorder, the harsh polemics of black revolt and white repression have been seen and heard before in this country.

It is time now to end the destruction and the violence, not only in the streets of the ghetto but in the lives of people.

Appendix

The Commission has already addressed itself to the need for immediate action at the local level. Because the city is the focus of racial disorder, the immediate responsibility rests on community leaders and local institutions. Yet the disorders are not simply a problem of the racial ghetto or the city. They are symptoms of social ills that have become endemic in our society and now affect every American.

None of us can escape the consequences of the continuing economic and social decay of the central city and the closely related problem of rural poverty. Only a greatly enlarged commitment to national action—compassionate, massive, and sustained, backed by the will and resources of the most powerful and the richest nation on this earth—can shape a future that is compatible with the historic ideals of American society.

It is this conviction that leads us, as a commission on civil disorders, to comment on the shape and dimension of the action that must be taken at the national level. While we do not claim competence to chart the details of programs within such complex and interrelated fields as employment, welfare, education, and housing, we do believe it is essential to set forth goals and to recommend strategies to reach these goals. Our aim is to impart our sense of the critical priorities. We discuss and recommend programs to illustrate the type and dimension of action needed.

Much has been accomplished in recent years to formulate new directions for national policy and new channels for national energy. Resources devoted to social programs have been greatly increased in many areas. Hence, few of our program suggestions are entirely novel. In some form, many are already in effect.

All this serves to underscore our basic conclusion: The need is not so much for the government to design new programs as it is for the nation to generate new will. Private enterprise, labor unions, the churches, the foundations, the universities—all our urban institutions—must deepen their involvement in the life of the city and their commitment to its revival and welfare.

Suggested Programs in Employment We are proposing programs in six areas: (1) Consolidating and concentrating employment efforts; (2) Opening the existing job structure; (3) Creating one million new jobs in the public sector in three years; (4) Creating one million new jobs in the private sector in three years; (5) Developing urban and rural poverty areas; (6) Encouraging business ownership in the ghetto.

Suggested Programs in Education We are suggesting programs in five areas: (1) Increasing efforts to eliminate *de facto* segregation: Among techniques commonly used to accomplish this at present in some areas are school pairing, busing, open enrollment, boundary changes, strategic use of site selection, enlargement of attendance areas, and consolidation of schools to overcome racial imbalance; (2) Providing quality education in ghetto schools; (3) Improving community–school relations; (4) Expanding opportunities for higher education; (5) Expanding opportunities for vocational education.

Suggested Programs in Welfare We recommend that programs be undertaken in two main areas: (1) In the overhauling of the existing categorical system of welfare so that it will provide more adequate levels of assistance on the basis of uniform national standards, reduce the burden on state and local government by financing assistance costs almost entirely with Federal funds, create new incentives to work, eliminate welfare features that cause hardship and dependency, and improve family planning and other social services to welfare recipients; (2) In developing a national system of income supplementation to provide a basic floor of economic and social security for all Americans.

Suggested Programs in Housing The Commission recommends programs in ten areas: (1) Provision of 600,000 low- and moderate-income housing units next year and six million units over the next five years; (2) An expanded and modified below-market interest rate program; (3) An expanded and modified rent supplement program and an ownership supplement program; (4) Federal write-down of interest rates on loans to private builders; (5) An expanded and more diversified public housing program; (6) An expanded Model Cities Program; (7) A reoriented and expanded urban renewal program; (8) Reform of obsolete building codes; (9) Enactment of a national, comprehensive, and enforceable open-occupancy law; (10) Reorientation of Federal housing programs to place more low- and moderate-income housing outside the ghetto areas.

Suggestions for Further Reading

Adoff, Arnold, ed. *Black on Black.* New York: The Macmillan Company, 1968.
   Commentaries by black Americans from the time of Frederick Douglass to the present.

Bardolph, Richard. *The Negro Vanguard.* New York: Vintage Books, 1961.
   Negro leadership from 1770 to the present.

Bennett, Lerone. *Before the Mayflower* (rev. ed.). Chicago: Johnson Publishing Company, 1962.
   An excellent history of the Negro in America.

———. *Confrontation: Black and White.* Chicago: Johnson Publishing Company, 1965.
   Perceptive and balanced social criticism.

———. *Black Power U.S.A.: The Human Side of Reconstruction 1867–1877.* Chicago: Johnson Publishing Company, 1967.
   A lively narrative based on sound historical research.

Blaustein, A. P., and Zangrando, R. L. *Civil Rights and the American Negro: A Documentary History.* New York: Washington Square Press, 1968.
   Authors supply background material where needed to explain social and historical situations that gave rise to the documents.

Bontemps, Arna. *One Hundred Years of Negro Freedom.* New

York: Dodd, Mead & Company, 1961.
  Story of the Negro struggle for full, free citizenship.

Bowen, David. *The Struggle Within.* New York: W. W. Norton & Company, 1965.
  Facts surrounding race relations from slavery times to the present.

Brown, Sterling, Davis, A. P., and Lee, Ulysses. *The Negro Caravan.* New York: Dryden Press, 1941.
  An anthology of writings by Negro authors, beginning with poems of the slave girl Phyllis Wheatley.

Chambers, Bradford, ed. *Chronicles of Negro Protest.* New York: Parents' Magazine Press, 1968.
  A background book documenting the history of Black Power.

Clark, Kenneth. *Dark Ghetto.* New York: Harper & Row, Publishers, 1965.
  A classic work by a leading American sociologist who was one of the most effective witnesses before the President's Advisory Commission on Civil Disorders.

Douglass, Frederick. *Life and Times of Frederick Douglass.* New York: Thomas Y. Crowell Company, 1966.

———. *The Mind and Heart of Frederick Douglass.* New York: Thomas Y. Crowell Company, 1968.
  The autobiography and the speeches of the antislavery leader, abridged by Barbara Ritchie.

Drisko, Carol F., and Toppin, E. A. *The Unfinished March.* Garden City: Doubleday & Company, 1967.
  A short, straightforward history of the Negro and racism in the United States between the Civil War and World War I.

Dumond, Dwight L. *Antislavery: The Crusade for Freedom in America.* Ann Arbor: University of Michigan Press, 1961.
  A history of the nineteenth century reform movement and its martyrs.

Evers, Mrs. Medgar, with Peters, William. *For Us, the Living.* Garden City: Doubleday and Company, 1967.
  At once an autobiography, a love story, and an account of the civil-rights movement.

Franklin, John Hope. *From Slavery to Freedom* (rev. ed.). New York: Alfred A. Knopf, 1967.

A deservedly popular general history of black Americans.

Frazier, E. Franklin. *The Negro in the United States* (rev. ed.). New York: The Macmillan Company, 1957.
    An excellent presentation of the sociological history of the Negro. A standard work.

Goldston, Robert. *The Negro Revolution.* New York: The Macmillan Company, 1968.
    A clear presentation of the sweep of Negro history and of racism.

Hernton, Calvin C. *White Papers for White Americans.* Garden City: Doubleday & Company, 1966.
    White middle-class myths about the Negro are examined.

Hughes, Langston and Meltzer, Milton. *A Pictorial History of the Negro in America* (rev. ed.). New York: Crown Publishers, 1968.
    An illustrated history of black Americans.

Lester, Julius. *To Be a Slave.* New York: The Dial Press, 1968.
    Narratives of men, women, and children who experienced slavery.

Marx, Gary T. *Protest and Prejudice.* New York: Harper & Row, Publishers, 1967.
    What the Negro thinks of himself and his situation in America is revealed in this survey of Negro opinion in 1964.

Meltzer, Milton. *Time of Trial, Time of Hope: The Negro in America, 1919–1941.* Garden City: Doubleday & Company, 1966.
    Clear, forceful delineation of the Negro's second-class status in America.

———. *In Their Own Words.* New York: Thomas Y. Crowell Company, 1967.
    Three volumes, in which Negroes tell their own history.

Morsbach, Mabel. *The Negro in American Life.* New York: Harcourt, Brace & World, 1967.
    Short, compact, comprehensive history of the Negro and his contributions to American life.

Nelson, Truman. *The Torture of Mothers.* Boston: Beacon Press, 1965.
    A dismaying chronicle of the nightmarish Harlem riot of 1964.

Redding, J. Saunders. *The Lonesome Road.* Garden City: Doubleday & Company, 1958.

An historical appraisal of the Negro's role in America. Well written and forceful.

———. *The Negro.* New York: Taplinger, 1967.
A good history.

Rose, Peter I. *They and We.* New York: Random House, 1963.
A short, concise, clear exposition of racial and ethnic relations in the United States.

Schechter, Betty. *The Peaceable Revolution.* Boston: Houghton Mifflin Company, 1963.
A dramatic picture of nonviolent resistance.

Silberman, Charles E. *Crisis in Black and White.* New York: Random House, 1964.
An honest attempt to see American society as it is.

Stratton, Madeline Robinson. *Negroes Who Helped Build America.* Boston: Ginn and Company, 1965.
Biographies of well-known and some not-so-well-known Negroes who have achieved distinction in America.

Wills, Gary. *The Second Civil War: Arming for Armageddon.* Cleveland: The World Publishing Company, 1968.
Wills's survey of riot cities following the 1967 disturbances brings insight and deeper understanding to the problems— but no clear-cut solutions.

Woodward, C. Vann. *The Strange Career of Jim Crow* (rev. ed.). New York: Oxford University Press, 1966.
Essential for an understanding of segregation in the United States.

Supplemental Studies for the National Advisory Commission on Civil Disorders. July 1968.
The three studies—*Racial Attitudes in Fifteen Cities, American Institutions in the Ghetto,* and *Who Riots?*—were conducted by research groups at the University of Michigan, the Johns Hopkins University, and Columbia University. Although the studies are still in progress and not complete, the preliminary reports contribute importantly to an understanding of the tensions and dissensions in riot areas.
For sale by Superintendent of Documents, United States Government Printing Office, Washington, D.C. 20402. $1.50.

Index

Abolitionists, 79, 82
Alienation of youth, 70
American Moral Reform Society, 81
Attucks, Crispus, 76

Birmingham, Ala., 20, 111, 120, 121
Black Muslims, 119, 125
Black Panther Party, 128
Black Power, 70, 125-26, 128, 129-30, 131, 233, 234
Black racism, 70
Brown v. Board of Education, 110-11

Carmichael, Stokely, 31
Cavanagh, Jerome, 39, 41, 42, 44
Cervantes, Alfonso J., quoted, 196
Chicago, Ill., 24, 28-30, 93, 139, 168, 170; crime rates in, 162; riot in (1919), 99-100, 243; riot in (1966), 28, 30
CIO (Congress of Industrial Organizations), 104
Cities: decrease in tax dollars for, 225; enrichment policy for, 219, 220, 221, 229-38; integration policy for, 219, 220-21, 238-40; present policies for, 219, 220-29; private capital investment in, 226; problems of, 188-90, 192-93, 195-98; programs recommended for, 198-201; projection of population of (1985), 226; prospects for, 218-43

City councils, 200
City-manager concept, 197
Civil disorders, 57-61, 69, 120, 169, 184, 190, 211; community response to, 208-11; recommendations for control of incidents leading to, 210; *see also* Riots; Violence
Civil Rights Act of 1875, 88, 90
Civil Rights Act of 1964, 120, 121
Civil Rights Commision, 111, 235
Civil-rights movement, 22, 69, 111-19
Civil War, 86, 93, 137; Negroes in, 84
Clark, Kenneth B., quoted, 204, 243
Cleveland, Ohio, 22, 30, 157
Commission, *see* National Advisory Commission on Civil Disorders
Compromise of 1850, 82
Congress of Racial Equality, *see* CORE
Constitutional Convention, 77
CORE (Congress of Racial Equality), 22, 107-09, 110, 117, 119, 123, 124, 128, 129
Crime, in ghetto, 66, 157, 158, 160-64, 204
Crisis, 100, 104
Cuffee, Paul, 79-81

Declaration of Independence, 76

Delany, Martin R., 81
Depression of 1930s, 102, 104, 137
Detroit, Mich., 13, 26, 34, 73, 101, 195, 196, 203; Federal programs in, 39, 41; Fire Department of, 43, 44; National Guard in, during 1967 riot, 44, 47, 48, 49, 50, 52, 53; Negro population of, 38, 39; Police Department of, 34, 41, 42; and police brutality, charges of, 50; property damage in (1967), 224; riot in (1943), 109-10; riot in (1967), 41-53, 214; schools in, 38, 39; union structure in, 38, 39; urban renewal in, 36, 41
Direct-action tactics, 120, 125, 131
Douglass, Frederick, quoted, 82
Draft Riots, New York, 84, 86
Drew, Charles, 106
Drug addiction, 158
Du Bois, W. E. B., 93, 94, 100, 104, 128

East St. Louis, Ill., 96, 98
Emancipation Proclamation, 84
Enrichment policy, for cities, 219, 220, 221, 229-38
Evers, Medgar, 120

Fair Employment Practices Commission (FEPC), 107
Farmer, James, 117
Federal Bureau of Investigation, 54, 209
Federal Disaster Act, 215
Fellowship of Reconciliation, 109, 110
Fifteenth Amendment, 88, 89
Fourteenth Amendment, 88
Freedom Democratic Party, Mississippi, 123
Freedom Ride, 110

Gandhi, Mahatma, 109
Garnishment practices, 173
Garvey, Marcus, 101-02, 128
Ghetto, 66, 73, 116, 126, 160-75, 190, 192, 193, 195, 201; civil disorders in, 169; crime in, 160-64; disease in, 164-65; estimated growth of (1975), 233; expanded employment of residents of, 200-01; fatherless families in, 66, 156-57; meetings of legislative bodies with residents of, 200; merchants in, 169, 171, 173, 174, 175; police in, 190, 192, 203-04, 206-07, 210; sanitation in, 166-69, 192; unemployment and underemployment in, 60, 148-53, 155, 223; youth in, 70, 153, 157, 207, 230; *see also* Negroes, in central cities
Girardin, Ray, 41, 42

Harlem, 24, 73, 110, 180, 201, 243
Harlem Renaissance, 100, 128
Health insurance, 166
Henderson, Vivian, quoted, 123-24
Housing: enrichment programs for, 237; freedom of choice in, 240; laws for open, 232

Illegitimacy rate, among nonwhite women, 158
Index crimes, in ghetto, 160, 163-64
Insurance: damage, 214-15; health, 166
Integration: denounced by Black Power advocates, 234; policy of, for cities, 219, 220-21, 238-40; and quality education, 235-37, 240

Jamestown, first Negroes at, 75
Jefferson, Thomas, 77, 78
Jim Crow laws, 92, 94-96
Johnson, Lyndon B., 121
Journey of Reconciliation, 110
Justice, "assembly-line," 211
Juvenile delinquency rates, in disadvantaged Negro areas, 158

Kansas–Nebraska Act of 1854, 82
Kennedy, John F., 120, 121
King, Martin Luther, Jr., 111, 113, 114, 116, 121
Ku Klux Klan, 22, 88, 89, 99

Labor unions, Negroes excluded from, 92
Lader, Lawrence, quoted, 84, 86
Law enforcement, 203-07, 208-11
Legal service, for poor, 199
Lincoln, Abraham, 84
Los Angeles, Calif., 25-28, 109, 157
Lynchings of Negroes, 22, 92, 99

Malcolm X, 125
Mayors: Federal and state assistance for, 200; leadership by, 201

Medicare, 165
Meredith, James, 35, 125
Messenger, 101
Mississippi, 121, 125, 139; Freedom Democratic Party in, 123; Freedom Ride to, 117; Negro voter registration in, 123
Model Cities Program, 221, 229
Montgomery, Ala., 111, 116
Moses, Robert, 123
Moynihan, Daniel P., quoted, 148

NAACP (National Association for the Advancement of Colored People), 94, 100-01, 104-05, 111-13, 116, 117, 119, 126
Narcotics addiction, 158
National Advisory Commission on Civil Disorders, 13-15, 54, 152, 168, 169, 210, 211, 214, 215, 229, 237, 243; judicial reforms recommended by, 211, 213-14; and news media, views on, 215, 216-17; programs recommended by, for central cities, 198-201, 206-07, 210; quoted, 54, 211, 213, 215, 216-17
National Association for the Advancement of Colored People, *see* NAACP
National Negro Movement, 81, 128
National States Rights Party, 30
National Urban League, 101, 102, 117
Negro population of U.S., 134-37, 139-40, 218, 228, 229, 233
Negro Revolt, 114
Negroes: arrest rate of, 164; birth rate of, 136, 137, 139; and Black Power, 70, 125-26, 128, 129-30, 131, 233, 234; business enterprise by, 126, 128; in central cities, 140, 145, 148, 218, 225, 228, 229, 233, 242 (*see also* Ghetto); in Civil War, 84; and cooperatives, 128; death rate of, 136, 165; during Depression of 1930s, 102, 104, 137; discrimination against, 65, 66, 74, 90, 104, 109, 131, 141-42, 145, 152, 155, 166, 176, 177-78, 192; as elected officials, 196; and European immigrants, comparisons between, 176-78, 180-182, 184, 185; excluded from labor unions, 92; in ghetto, *see* Ghetto; grievances of, and civil disorders, 58-60, 61; historical sketch of, 74-105; and housing, 141-45, 232, 237, 240; income levels of, 146-47, 156-57; job-training programs for, 128, 200; life expectancy of, 165; lynchings of, 22, 92, 99; middle-class, 130, 141, 146, 147, 184, 229, 232, 233; migration of, 65, 131, 134, 137-39, 233; militant, 61, 70, 113, 124, 130; and New Deal, 104; and police, 73, 190, 192, 203-204, 206-207, 210; and political machines, 180; during Reconstruction, 88-89; in Revolutionary War, 76-77; segregation of, 65, 66, 90, 96, 117, 144, 145, 180, 181-82, 195, 218, 220, 221, 228; as slaves, 75-76, 77-82, 84, 181; unemployment and underemployment of, 60, 148-49, 151-53, 155, 177, 223; upper-income, 146, 147; and voter-registration campaigns, 123, 126; and white liberals, 131; and white racism, 64-66, 69, 70, 73, 125, 130, 234; in World War I, 98-99; in World War II, 106-107; young, 60, 70, 152, 153, 157, 207, 223, 230
Neighborhood action task forces, 198
New Deal, 104, 110
New York, N.Y., 22-24, 168, 170, 173, 174, 180, 228; anti-Negro riots in (1900), 92; Draft Riots in (1863), 84, 86
Newark, N.J., 13, 34, 73, 84, 201, 214, 224
Niagara Movement, 93, 94

Oklahoma "grandfather clause," 94
Old Age Assistance Program, 165
Open-housing laws, 232

Pan-Africanism, 128
Parks, Rosa, 111
Patricelli, Robert, quoted, 168-69
Plessy v. Ferguson, 90
Polarization, and ghetto, 228, 237
Police, and Negroes, 73, 190, 192, 203-204, 206-207, 210
Police brutality, charges of, 35, 50, 73

Poll tax, 105
Population of U.S.: Negro, 134-37, 139-40, 218, 228, 229, 233; white, 135, 136, 140
Poverty: "culture" of, 158; level of, defined by Social Security Administration, 153; War on, 221, 229-30
Prosser, Gabriel, 79

Racial transition, in central-city neighborhoods, 142-44
Racism: black, 70; white, 64-66, 69, 70, 73, 125, 130, 234
Randolph, A. Philip, 101, 107, 120
Reconstruction, 88
Red Cross, 106
Revolutionary War, Negroes in, 76-77
Riot manual, FBI, 209
Riots: anti-Negro, 78, 84, 86, 92, 96-98, 99-100; of 1963-64, 22-24, of 1965, 25-26, of 1966, 26-30, of 1967, 13, 30-33, 34-53; "typical," 56-61; see also Civil disorders; Violence
Romney, George, 44
Roosevelt, Franklin D., 107

School segregation, 105, 237; abolished by Supreme Court, 111, 113; de facto, 120
SCLC (Southern Christian Leadership Conference), 113, 116, 117, 119, 121
Scott, Dred, 82
Segregation, 65, 66, 90, 96, 117, 144, 145, 180, 181-82, 195, 218, 220, 221, 228; in Schools, see School segregation
Separatism, 242; and Black Power, 130, 233, 234
Sheridan, Philip H., quoted, 86
Sit-ins, student, 114
Slavery, Negro, 75-76, 77-82, 84, 130, 181
SNCC (Student Nonviolent Coordinating Committee), 30-31, 116, 117, 119, 123, 124, 128, 129
Southern Christian Leadership Conference, see SCLC
Springfield, Ill., anti-Negro riot in (1908), 92-93
State government, role of, 201
Student Nonviolent Coordinating Committee, see SNCC
Supreme Court, 89, 90, 94, 105, 110, 113, 114; in *Brown v. Board of Education*, 110-11; in Dred Scott decision, 82; and Oklahoma "grandfather clause," 94; in *Plessy v. Ferguson*, 90
Sweet, Ossian, 100

Thirteenth Amendment, 88
Throckmorton, John L., 48, 52
Tokenism, 125
Tubman, Harriet, quoted, 81
Turner, Nat, 79

Uncle Tom's Cabin, 82
Underground railroad, 81
UNIA (Universal Negro Improvement Association), 102
Unions, Negroes excluded from, 92
Universal Negro Improvement Association, see UNIA
Urban League, National, 101, 102, 117

Vesey, Denmark, 79
Violence: climate of, 69, 73; racist appeals to, 70; retaliatory, 126, 129; see also Civil disorders; Riots

War on Poverty, 221, 229-30
Washington, Booker T., 93, 94, 101, 128, 130
Washington, George, 78
Washington, D.C., 99, 107, 158, 171, 173, 174; March on, 120-21
Watts district, in Los Angeles, 26, 73, 157, 201, 214, 243
White Citizens' Council, 114
White middle class, in suburbs, 65, 144, 189, 218, 232, 242
White population, in U.S., 135, 136, 140
White racism, 64-66, 69, 70, 73, 125, 130, 234
World War I, Negroes in, 98-99
World War II, Negroes in, 106-07

Young, Whitney M., Jr., 117

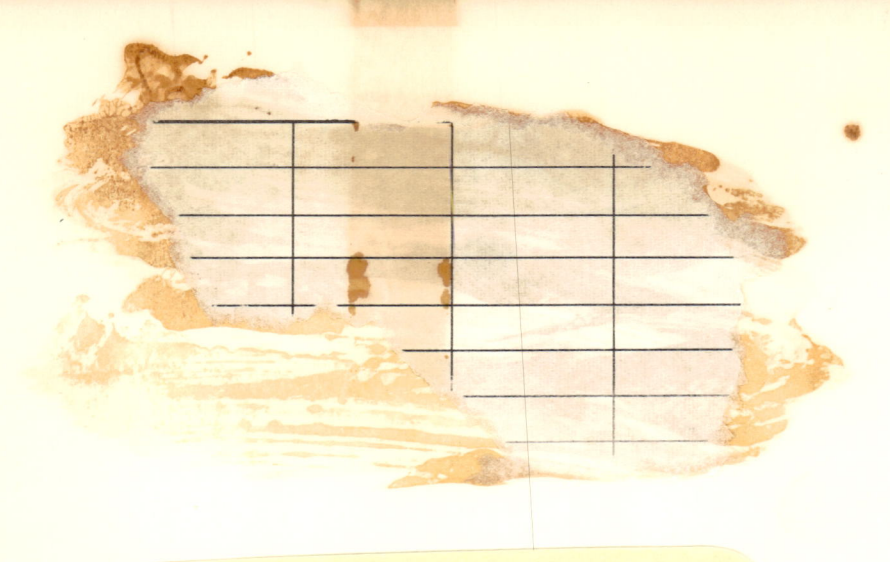

```
301.18                                    4824
   R      RITCHIE, BARBARA
          THE RIOT REPORT
```

Elmsford Public Schools
ELMSFORD, NEW YORK
ALEXANDER HAMILTON HIGH SCHOOL LIBRARY

RULES

1. Books may be kept two weeks and may be renewed once for the same period, except "reserved" books and magazines.

2. A fine of five cents for the first day, and one cent a day thereafter will be charged on each book which is not returned according to the above rule. No book will be issued to any person incurring such a fine until it has been paid.

3. All injuries to books beyond reasonable wear and all losses shall be made good to the satisfaction of the Librarian.

4. Each borrower is held responsible for all books drawn on his card and for all fines accruing on same.

Alexander Hamilton High School
301.18 RIT
United States.
The riot report :a shortened version of

3 0001 0000 1552